Whitaker House Books by E. M. Bounds

A PLACE CALLED HEAVEN

E. M. BOUNDS

WHITAKER
HOUSE

Publisher's Note: The author's selection of Bible versions has been retained whenever possible, including the Revised Version when it was originally cited. The text of this book, however, has been edited for the modern reader. Words, expressions, and sentence structure have been updated for clarity and readability.

Unless otherwise indicated, all Scripture quotations are taken from the King James Version (KJV) of the Holy Bible. Scripture quotations marked (RV) are taken from the Revised Version of the Holy Bible.

A PLACE CALLED HEAVEN
updated edition
Previously published as *Inside Heaven's Gates* and
Catching a Glimpse of Heaven

ISBN-13: 978-0-88368-958-5
ISBN-10: 0-88368-958-8
Printed in the United States of America
© 1985, 2003 by Whitaker House

Whitaker House
1030 Hunt Valley Circle
New Kensington, PA 15068
www.whitakerhouse.com

Library of Congress Cataloging-in-Publication Data
Bounds, Edward M. (Edward McKendree), 1835–1913.
A place called heaven / E.M. Bounds.—Updated ed.
        p.   cm.
Rev. ed. of: Inside heaven's gates. 1999; Catching a glimpse of heaven. 1985.
ISBN 0-88368-958-8 (trade pbk.)
1. Heaven—Christianity. I. Bounds, Edward M. (Edward McKendree), 1835–1913. Inside heaven's gates. II. Bounds, Edward M. (Edward McKendree), 1835–1913. Catching a glimpse of heaven. III. Title.
BT846.3.B68 2003
236'.24—dc22   2003017958

2 3 4 5 6 7 8 9 10 11 12 **ᵾ** 15 14 13 12 11 10 09 08 07

Contents

Introduction

While pastoring in Atlanta in 1905, I was informed that there was an apostolic man of prayer in Georgia who would aid the church in attaining a high altitude in spiritual things. I sent a letter asking Mr. Bounds to come to our convention for ten days of preaching.

We expected to see a man of imposing physique, but when he came we discovered that he was only about five and a half feet tall. In him we met one of the greatest saints that, in our humble opinion, has appeared on the spiritual horizon in the last hundred years.

He spoke on prayer the first afternoon. No one seemed to be particularly impressed. The next morning at 4 a.m., we were amazed to hear him engaged in the most wonderful prayer we have ever listened to—a prayer that seemed to take in both heaven and earth. All his sermons were about prayer and heaven.

Not one morning during his stay did he fail to pray. He did not care about the protests of the other occupants of his room at being awakened at that unheard-of hour. No man could have made more melting appeals for lost souls and backslidden ministers than did Bounds. Tears ran down his face as he pleaded for all of us in that room. I know of no other man on earth today, who, if he had followed the same experiment at the same place and in the same room, would have gone away undefeated. But Bounds was all-powerful, all-commanding, all-victorious, once he knew his cause was just.

After that convention we took him into our hearts and never let him go. In answer to prayer, he was sent to settle and establish me in the things of God that are foremost and supreme—prayer, preaching, and the study of the Bible.

We were constantly with him, in prayer and preaching, for eight precious years. We never heard him utter a foolish word. He was one of the most intense eagles of God that ever penetrated the spiritual sky.

—Homer W. Hodge

1

Heaven, a Place

*IF GOD HAD TOLD ME SOME TIME AGO THAT HE WAS
ABOUT TO MAKE ME AS HAPPY AS I COULD BE IN THIS
WORLD, AND THEN HAD TOLD ME THAT HE SHOULD
BEGIN BY CRIPPLING ME IN ALL MY LIMBS, AND REMOV-
ING ME FROM ALL MY USUAL SOURCES OF ENJOYMENT,
I SHOULD HAVE THOUGHT IT A VERY STRANGE MODE OF
ACCOMPLISHING HIS PURPOSE. AND YET, HOW IS HIS
WISDOM MANIFEST EVEN IN THIS! FOR IF YOU SHOULD
SEE A MAN SHUT UP IN A CLOSE ROOM, IDOLIZING A
SET OF LAMPS AND REJOICING IN THEIR LIGHT, AND YOU
WISHED TO MAKE HIM TRULY HAPPY, YOU WOULD BEGIN
BY BLOWING OUT ALL HIS LAMPS; AND THEN THROW
OPEN THE SHUTTERS TO LET IN THE LIGHT OF HEAVEN.*
—SAMUEL RUTHERFORD

Heaven is a place. It is not from the region of
fancy but a point in the realm of the actual
and local. The facts are that death does not
end all, that death cannot end all, that man must exist
through all eternity, and that the future may be one

of unutterable bliss. These facts may have many interpretations, but that should not be our primary concern. Heaven does not float around. It is not made of thin air. It is a real country, climate, and sacred home, where our affinities draw us. Divine assurance settles and fixes the fact.

Theoretically, it is possible for heaven to be a state of being rather than a concrete reality. In its location and grasp, heaven may be airy and volatile. But the Bible teaches that it is a place. It is a settled city rather than a pilgrim state, unsettled and temporary.

The strong argument for heaven as a place centers in, and clusters about, Jesus. The man Jesus, in human form, has a place assigned Him—a high place.

Wherefore God also hath highly exalted him, and given him a name which is above every name: that at the name of Jesus every knee should bow, of things in heaven, and things in earth, and things under the earth; and that every tongue should confess that Jesus Christ is Lord, to the glory of God the Father. (Phil. 2:9–11)

He raised him from the dead, and set him at his own right hand in the heavenly places, far above all principality, and power, and might, and dominion, and every name that is named, not only in this world, but also in that which is to come: and hath put all things under his feet, and gave him to be the head over all things to the church, which is his body, the fulness of him that filleth all in all. (Eph. 1:20–23)

This excellence and dignity indicates a place of high honor—the best, most royal in the heavenly world.

God, who at sundry times and in divers manners spake in time past unto the fathers by the prophets, hath in these last days spoken unto us by his Son, whom he hath appointed heir of all things, by whom also he made the worlds; who being the brightness of his glory, and the express image of his person, and upholding all things by the word of his power, when he had by himself purged our sins, sat down on the right hand of the Majesty on high. (Heb. 1:1–3)

These verses all speak of Jesus' place in God's many-mansioned country. *"Who is gone into heaven, and is on the right hand of God; angels and authorities and powers being made subject unto him"* (1 Peter 3:22).

These are descriptions of Christ's exaltation and location. They are descriptions of a place. Jesus wants us with Him. He wants us to see and share His glory. He dwells in a place—a place that honors and glorifies His person and presence. His business is not to be enthroned and receive honor, but to prepare a place for us.

Father, I will that they also, whom thou hast given me, be with me where I am; that they may behold my glory, which thou hast given me. (John 17:24)

The Journey's End

In the Bible, heaven is represented as a place, in contrast with earth. The earth is a place, but it is unstable, insecure, and fleeting. Heaven is stable, secure, and eternal. *"For here have we no continuing city, but we seek one to come"* (Heb. 13:14).

The contrast between earth and heaven is remarkable! Earth is merely a pilgrim's stay, a pilgrim's journey, a pilgrim's tent. Heaven is a city—permanent, God-planned, God-built—whose foundations are as stable as God's throne.

By faith Abraham, when he was called to go out into a place which he should after receive for an inheritance, obeyed; and he went out, not knowing whither he went. By faith he sojourned in the land of promise, as in a strange country, dwelling in tabernacles with Isaac and Jacob, the heirs with him of the same promise: for he looked for a city which hath foundations, whose builder and maker is God. (Heb. 11:8–10)

The Bible reveals heaven as a place. It is measured off with appointed boundaries like an actual walled city. It has its inside and its outside. Heaven is inside the city while hell is outside. *"For without are dogs, and sorcerers, and whoremongers, and murderers, and idolaters, and whosoever loveth and maketh a lie"* (Rev. 22:15).

Heaven is a place. It is not airy, impalpable, or without a specific location. *"I go,"* said Jesus, *"to prepare a **place** for you"* (John 14:2, emphasis added).

Place means locality, something settled. Heaven has its boundaries on God's map. Jesus declared that there are *"many mansions"* (John 14:2) in His Father's house. Out of God's many homes, one home was to belong to the disciples; a place, a home prepared for them. This was a solace to the disciples, saddened as they were by Jesus' approaching departure.

"To prepare a place for [them]*"* was the purpose for Christ's leaving. Nothing can be simpler, more explicit, more downright honest than this revelation to them of Christ's purpose and plans. He essentially said, "Earth is a place where we have been abiding. We can abide together no longer here, but God has many other abiding places. I go to select one of these places for you. When it is ready, I will come and take you there. Then we will be together in place as well as in spirit, *'that where I am, there ye may be also'"* (v. 3).

Our Preparation and Inheritance

Jesus used the phrase, *"prepare a place."* It means to make the necessary preparations and get everything ready. It is an illustration drawn from the eastern custom of sending people before kings to level the roads and make them passable. Jesus is our pioneer, gone to prepare heaven for us. He will ensure that it is made ready.

Heaven's earthly equivalent was Canaan, a prepared place. Israel did not have to pioneer the way, build cities, or homes. Homes and cities were already built for them. Nothing was required except that they simply enter in, possess, and enjoy. As Canaan was but a feeble type of heaven, so its preparation was but a faint shadow of the preparation that is made for us in heaven. Canaan was man-made, but heaven is God-built. Its homes are not made with hands, but stand eternal in the heavens.

As Jesus Christ drew near to the end, important things engaged His attention. He had to commit to His disciples the interests of His kingdom. Heaven was all-important. Heaven was to be kept in eye and heart all the time. Their deep spiritual life, their personal holiness, and their conscious abiding in Christ were crucial. Christ spoke of the importance of Christ-life and Christlikeness in His last sacred words.

What could be clearer, more hope-giving, or more conclusive than the utterance of Christ on the verge of His going away? His disciples were sorrowfully impressed, deeply touched, and heavily depressed by the fact of His leaving them. In response, He challenged their faith in Himself and linked Himself inseparably as the object of their faith with God.

The Sight of Saints

Peter viewed heaven as a place, an inheritance to be sought for, and a possession awaiting us. He was enraptured by the glorious vision of heaven.

Blessed be the God and Father of our Lord Jesus Christ, which according to his abundant mercy

hath begotten us again unto a lively hope by the resurrection of Jesus Christ from the dead, to an inheritance incorruptible, and undefiled, and that fadeth not away, reserved in heaven for you, who are kept by the power of God through faith unto salvation ready to be revealed in the last time.
(1 Peter 1:3–5)

This is no impalpable state without location, nor merely a name without a reality. Heaven is definitely located, named definitely, and definitely described.

John had a picture of heaven that located it. The picture is for charm, comfort, and strength.

After this I beheld, and, lo, a great multitude, which no man could number, of all nations, and kindreds, and people, and tongues, stood before the throne, and before the Lamb, clothed with white robes, and palms in their hands; and cried with a loud voice, saying, Salvation to our God which sitteth upon the throne, and unto the Lamb. And all the angels stood round about the throne, and about the elders and the four beasts, and fell before the throne on their faces, and worshipped God, saying, Amen: blessing, and glory, and wisdom, and thanksgiving, and honour, and power, and might, be unto our God for ever and ever. Amen. And one of the elders answered, saying unto me, What are these which are arrayed in white robes? and whence came they? And I said unto him, Sir, thou knowest. And he said to me, These are they which came out of great tribulation, and have washed their robes, and made

15

them white in the blood of the Lamb. Therefore are they before the throne of God, and serve him day and night in his temple: and he that sitteth on the throne shall dwell among them. They shall hunger no more, neither thirst any more; neither shall the sun light on them, nor any heat. For the Lamb which is in the midst of the throne shall feed them, and shall lead them unto living fountains of waters: and God shall wipe away all tears from their eyes. (Rev. 7:9–17)

"To day shalt thou be with me in paradise" (Luke 23:43) was the answer of Jesus to the prayer of the dying thief. *"Through the gates into the city"* (Rev. 22:14) represents a place. *"Absent from the body...to be present with the Lord"* (2 Cor. 5:8) also indicates locality. Elijah and Enoch were in their bodies when they went to be with the Lord. (See 2 Kings 2:11; Genesis 5:24.)

The future of the saints will not be impalpable and transitory, but defined, limited, and real—as soul and body will be real. The glorified will not be pilgrims, transient visitors, or tenants, but settled, permanent, walled, and established through eternity by deed—signed, sealed, and recorded. There will be no renters or lessees in heaven; everyone will be property- and home-owners. Heaven's patent is issued to guarantee right and title. In fact it is ours before we get there. It is reserved for us and guarded for us; our names of ownership are engraved and jeweled on our heavenly home.

A House Not Made with Hands

Heaven is a house, a *"house not made with hands, eternal in the heavens"* (2 Cor. 5:1). In this the apostle drew a contrast between a tent, its frailty and its temporary nature, and the permanence of heaven. *"For we know,"* said the apostle, *"that if our earthly house of this tabernacle were dissolved, we have a building of God, an house not made with hands, eternal in the heavens"* (v. 1).

All earthly houses, however beautiful, costly, and enduring they may be, are made with earthly hands and are subject to decay. The marks of their death are on them, laid in their very foundations. The houses of heaven are God-built and are as enduring and incorruptible as their Builder. After the resurrection, our bodies will be transfigured according to the model of Christ's glorious body. The transfiguration will refine and spiritualize the substance of our bodies, but we will still require houses to lodge us, as we do now.

What houses they will be! They will be fitted for every use, employment, and enjoyment of the heavenly citizens. These habitations will be worthy of God, their Builder, reflecting honor on and bringing glory to Him by their untold beauty, magnificence, and grandeur. Whatever Paul meant when he chose the word *house*, whether it is used to signify the glorious bodies that will be the habitations of our spirits, or it refers to some glorious structure outside of ourselves, fitted for home uses, as our houses are, it is all the same God-built mansion for spirit, or for body and spirit immortalized. It is *a building of God...not made with hands, eternal in the heavens."* It will be for us; we will be in it. A thing of beauty and joy forever and ever, amen!

In 2 Corinthians Paul again asserted the security and confidence of heaven: *"We are always confident, knowing that, whilst we are at home in the body, we are absent from the Lord"* (2 Cor. 5:6).

Home is always a place, the heart's place, the place where our longings draw us, and around which sweet memories cluster.

Paul was caught up into paradise, into the third heaven. The passages in this chapter and others have in them, in intention and spirit, a place. Lazarus was carried by the angels and located in Abraham's bosom. (See Luke 16:22.)

In the Bible it is taken for granted that heaven is a place—stable, enduring, all attractive—in contrast with the veering nature and transitory conditions of our earthly sojourn. If the description in John's revelation is an accurate description of the material aspects of heaven, the place is one of matchless and exquisite beauty, *"incorruptible, and undefiled, and that fadeth not away"* (1 Peter 1:4).

Stephen, the first martyr, was a man full of faith and the Holy Spirit. In the presence of a cruel, murderous death and an infuriated mob, he had the sight and calm of heaven.

But he, being full of the Holy Ghost, looked up stedfastly into heaven, and saw the glory of God, and Jesus standing on the right hand of God, and said, Behold, I see the heavens opened, and the Son of man standing on the right hand of God. Then they cried out with a loud voice, and stopped their ears, and ran upon him with one accord, and cast him out of the city, and stoned him: and the witnesses laid down their clothes at a young man's feet, whose name was Saul. And they stoned Stephen, calling upon God, and saying, Lord Jesus, receive my spirit. And he kneeled down, and cried with a loud voice, Lord, lay not this sin to their charge. And when he had said this, he fell asleep. (Acts 7:55–60)

Revealing the Kingdom

Jesus declared, *"I came down from heaven"* (John 6:42). We can learn much of heaven from Him. From heaven He came; for heaven He suffered. In heaven He lived; to heaven He returned. Born in heaven, living in heaven, breathing the air of heaven, speaking the language of heaven, longing for heaven; it would be strange if He did not speak much of heaven.

Using familiar language, He constantly emphasized that heaven is a place. What are the words in his memorable conversation with Nicodemus but a contrast of places—earth and heaven?

If I have told you earthly things, and ye believe not, how shall ye believe, if I tell you of heavenly things? And no man hath ascended up to heaven, but he that came down from heaven, even the Son of man which is in heaven. (John 3:12–13)

We are well assured that we will hear much from His lips of heaven. He began His Beatitudes, *"Blessed are the poor in spirit: for theirs is the kingdom of heaven"* (Matt. 5:3).

The Sermon on the Mount, among Jesus' first utterances, if not the very first, began with heaven. He taught us to let our light shine that we may glorify our Father in heaven and that, unless our righteousness exceeds the righteousness of the scribes and Pharisees, we will not enter into the kingdom of heaven (Matt. 5:16, 20). So Jesus began His divine mission and marvelous career with heaven accepted and recognized as a matter of course. His first preaching was saturated with the principles of heaven. *"Repent,"* Jesus said, *"for the kingdom of heaven is at hand"* (Matt. 4:17).

The first utterance of Jesus' first sermon was a beatitude of the kingdom of heaven. The diamond of character is, *"Blessed are the pure in heart: for they shall see God"* (Matt. 5:8). This includes seeing, knowing, and loving God, but it finds its full realization in heaven. To see God, to see Him in everything, in every tear that dims the eye or breaks the heart—that is heaven begun on earth. *"For now we see through a glass, darkly; but then face to face: now I know in part; but then shall I know even as also I am known"* (1 Cor. 13:12).

Jesus helped us to understand children and their character, and we see the child's inheritance, *"if children, then heirs"* (Rom. 8:17). *"Blessed are the peacemakers: for they shall be called the children of God"* (Matt. 5:9).

The next Beatitude reads, *"Blessed are they which are persecuted for righteousness' sake: for theirs is the kingdom of heaven"* (Matt. 5:10). This leads the way to the last:

> *Blessed are ye, when men shall revile you, and persecute you, and shall say all manner of evil against you falsely, for my sake. Rejoice, and be exceeding glad: for great is your reward in heaven: for so persecuted they the prophets which were before you.* (vv. 11–12)

Discipleship—Conduct and Character

In His first call to discipleship, Jesus stimulated and connected that call with all the alluring weight, comfort, and hope of heaven. Heaven is at the foundation of the system of Jesus, its first thought, brightest hope, and strongest faith. Jesus told His disciples that their Father dwells in heaven—a place worthy of being the abode of God—and they were to reflect glory on their Father in heaven.

The righteousness of Christ's followers must exceed the righteousness of the scribes and Pharisees or else the glories of heaven will not be theirs. The commonplace, popular piety will not bring heaven. Heaven, in the teaching of Jesus, is God's

21

throne. Earth is His footstool. As the throne excels in honor, character, and material, and uses the footstool, so heaven excels earth. How much, who can tell?

Christ would not let it out of His disciples' minds that their Father was in heaven, a place defined and located; that they were His children; and that they were to be like Him—to share His character, to imitate His conduct, and to share His heaven. Similarly, He shows us constantly that heaven is His home. The Father's character must be His children's character; the Father's conduct, His children's conduct; the Father's place, His children's place; the Father's home, His children's home.

Ye have heard that it hath been said, Thou shalt love thy neighbour, and hate thine enemy. But I say unto you, Love your enemies, bless them that curse you, do good to them that hate you, and pray for them which despitefully use you, and persecute you; that ye may be the children of your Father which is in heaven: for he maketh his sun to rise on the evil and on the good, and sendeth rain on the just and on the unjust. For if ye love them which love you, what reward have ye? do not even the publicans the same? And if ye salute your brethren only, what do ye more than others? do not even the publicans so? Be ye therefore perfect, even as your Father which is in heaven is perfect. (Matt. 5:43–48)

Jesus even prefaced descriptions of our duties with an emphasis on heaven as our Father's home.

Almsgiving, prayer, and fasting take their meaning and their obligation from *Our Father which art in heaven*" (Matt. 6:9).

Where Is Your Treasure?

Heaven is not only the home of God, but it is also to be the pattern after which earth is fashioned. Earth ought to look to heaven, its harmony, its beauty, and its ecstasy, all due to implicit obedience to God's will, and learn how to rival heaven. But instead earth is devoted to its own fashions and is even ready to forget the higher and holier place that it should emulate.

Jesus keeps the place, being, order, and beauty of heaven ever before us. He hangs the trappings and decorations of His abode all around the Father's house, saying, "Be like God. He is your Father. Children, be like your Father. Heaven is His home. Make your home like His."

Earth is unsafe, says Jesus. Thieves are here: Treasures are lost here. Moths are here: Finest silks and costliest robes are eaten. Rust is here: Richest jewels, finest gold, and costliest metals corrode. Heaven is a place, as surely as earth is a place, but it is a place of absolute safety. Thieves are never there. No robberies ever occur on its plains or in its cities. Moths are not known there. Its spotless robes have never been defiled by their touch. Its precious stones and metals do not know the corroding touch of rust. All is pure, polished, glittering, and forever secure. (See Matthew 6:19–20.) How emphatic and absolute the command for safety and obedience!

> *But lay up for yourselves treasures in heaven, where neither moth nor rust doth corrupt, and where thieves do not break through nor steal: for where your treasure is, there will your heart be also. The light of the body is the eye: if therefore thine eye be single, thy whole body shall be full of light. But if thine eye be evil, thy whole body shall be full of darkness. If therefore the light that is in thee be darkness, how great is that darkness!*
> (Matt. 6:20–23)

How the divine Teacher emphasized heaven! He wants our hearts to be there. The heart is the soul, the being, the man. Safety is in heaven. Put your values there only. Put your heart there. No tears are there to flood your heart, no sorrows there to break it, no losses there to grieve and embitter it. Put your heart in heaven, says Jesus, that it may be sweet, whole, and joyful. Put your treasures in heaven, says Jesus, and all will be light and clear, cloudless and strong. Don't divide your treasures between heaven and earth. If you do, the light will be mixed and confused and will make the darkness darker for the light lost in it. Don't divide between heaven and earth, says Jesus.

> *No man can serve two masters: for either he will hate the one, and love the other; or else he will hold to the one, and despise the other.* (Matt. 6:24)

Anxiety about food and clothing, the fears hidden in the womb of tomorrow, have mastered many a soul, bred fears, and uprooted faith. Jesus Christ shows that the cause of these anxieties is lack of faith in our Father in heaven. Their only infallible cure is an absorbing pursuit of heaven; *"But seek ye first the kingdom of God, and his righteousness; and all these things shall be added unto you"* (Matt. 6:33). He would quiet our anxieties by stressing the fact that our *"heavenly Father knoweth that ye have need of all these things"* (Matt. 6:32) and by linking us constantly with our Father's ability and concern for us. With heaven as His abode and ours, Jesus would calm our hearts and set them on heaven and its pursuits, which is impossible when earthly needs and necessaries bewilder and engross us. Heaven, to Jesus, is the real place, the Father's place and home.

Let others seek a home below,

Which flames devour, or waves o'erflow,

Be mine a happier lot, to own

A heavenly mansion near the throne.

Then fail this earth, let stars decline,

And sun and moon refuse to shine,

All nature sink and cease to be,

That heavenly mansion stands for me.

—William Hunter

2

Heaven, a City

IF CONTENTMENT WERE HERE, HEAVEN WERE NOT HEAVEN. I WONDER THAT EVER A CHILD OF GOD SHOULD HAVE A SAD HEART, CONSIDERING WHAT HIS LORD IS PREPARING FOR HIM. I KNOW NOT A THING WORTH THE BUYING BUT HEAVEN.

—SAMUEL RUTHERFORD

The city is of heavenly and divine birth, shaped and built by God in a heavenly mold with heavenly air about it. The heavenly life will come from God directly and will be heavenly, not earthly. Many earthly things, by chance, by happenings, and by direct purpose and appointment, shape our earthly lives; but in a direct and all-inclusive way, our heavenly lives will be from God, and the air and conditions of heaven will shape them. Earth will not be forgotten, but the former things will scarcely be remembered. The things of old will no longer be considered. They will be crowded out, overwhelmed, and retired by the magnificent grandeur and ever new and expanding glories of the present. Earth will be too little, its most sacred relations and most pleasing things all too poor, to come into mind in heaven.

And I saw a new heaven and a new earth: for the first heaven and the first earth were passed away; and there was no more sea. And I John saw the holy city, new Jerusalem, coming down from God out of heaven, prepared as a bride adorned for her husband. And I heard a great voice out of heaven saying, Behold, the tabernacle of God is with men, and he will dwell with them, and they shall be his people, and God himself shall be with them, and be their God. And God shall wipe away all tears from their eyes; and there shall be no more death, neither sorrow, nor crying, neither shall there be any more pain: for the former things are passed away. And he that sat upon the throne said, Behold, I make all things new.
(Rev. 21:1–5)

A transformed mind and memory, a purified thought and love, a transfigured body shining like a sun in noonday splendor, which has no eclipse and fears no night, a transfigured heaven and earth—this will be the saints' eternal inheritance.

God's power and glory makes all things new. A bride adorned for her husband, the marriage hour, and the bridal array are all emblems of the marriage of heaven and earth on their festal day. Perfect beauty, perfect taste, perfect joy will be heaven's honeymoon.

Receiving from the Source

The tabernacle refers to the place where God dwelled and manifested Himself to Moses. God will be essentially and immediately present with man in the heavenly world in a way in which He is not with man in this life. Man will draw his being and blessing directly from Him without the aid of intermediaries.

> *And I saw no temple therein: for the Lord God Almighty and the Lamb are the temple of it. And the city had no need of the sun, neither of the moon, to shine in it: for the glory of God did lighten it, and the Lamb is the light thereof.*
> (Rev. 21:22–23)

And again it is said, *"And they need no candle, neither light of the sun; for the Lord God giveth them light: and they shall reign for ever and ever"* (Rev. 22:5). In this life we cannot understand this. Secondary causes are the agencies through which God ministers to us in this world. In that higher life, these agencies will not intervene and hide God; instead we will see Him face to face. There will be no temple, no gorgeous service, no brilliant sun to shine. The glory of God, brighter than the light of a thousand suns, will be our light, and the mild sweet rays from the Lamb will cast their radiance over all the land, dispelling darkness and gloom and sorrow. *"For there shall be no night there"* (Rev. 21:25). And to make it strong and clear, it is declared a second time, *"And there shall be no night there"* (Rev. 22:5).

In heaven no tears will be shed, for God will wipe all tears from our eyes. *"And there shall be no more death, neither sorrow, nor crying, neither shall there be any more pain"* (Rev. 21:4). What a changed world! How difficult to imagine such a world! Tears are the sad heritage of this life. Sorrow and pain flow from a thousand sources to deepen, widen, and darken earth's sorrow. Our sweetest days give birth to our greatest sorrows. Our distresses often flow from our joys. Death reigns.

All this will be changed, and everything that gives pain and sorrow will be forever barred from heaven. God will shut it out. How bright the eyes undimmed by a tear! How strong and free our souls and bodies will be, utter and eternal strangers to pain! How bright and joyous our hearts will grow, with never a cloud or a sorrow. How full of richest and largest life—untouched by decay and unshadowed by death—heaven will be!

All things will be made new. There will be no marks of age, no common things, no freshened or repainted old things; all things will be absolutely new. There will be a new world, a new life, a new career, a new history, new environments, new conditions, new jobs, new destiny.

Worldly dreams, pictures, poetry, fiction, music—all have failed to give the faintest idea of that new world and its marvelous life, melody, and charms. To live there is rapture and indescribable ecstasy. Its climax is, *"He that overcometh shall inherit all things; and I will be his God, and he shall be my son"* (Rev. 21:7). It is the wonder and spectacle of angels.

Type and shadow, precept and promise, both in the Old and New Testaments, are tokens and seals of the saints' inheritance after death. No truth is more necessary to man or more in accordance with God's character, none more necessary to His glory, than the truth and doctrine of heaven. An eternal heaven of unsullied purity and unalloyed bliss through its endless years is a doctrine that enables man and honors God. The existence of heaven and its matchless perfection is a truth based upon the advent, the person, and the work of Jesus Christ, for He made heaven and is the way to it.

A Heavenly Metropolis

Heaven lies beyond this life. It is located in another world. The boundary line, death, must be crossed before its doors can be entered, before its happy land can be possessed and enjoyed. However, there are many lessons in the Bible that declare today, by word, figure, and picture, the fact of heaven.

Among the many varied illustrations by which the fact and nature of heaven are conveyed to us, that of a city is striking. It seems to convey more clearly and fully the idea and characteristic of that unseen and unknown land. A city teems with life. A city is a stirring scene. It contains life in its most opulent and strenuous form. Similarly, heaven is a city of life—so much so that it has never felt the touch or chill of death. Graves have never been dug there, cemeteries are unknown, tombstones and coffins are alien to that land. Heaven is a city of life—majestic, glorious life—a life that knows no tears, never feels sorrow, and never decays.

A city is a picture of closest union. Life in a city is forced into closest proximity. Unity, compactness, and nearness are essentials to city life.

Similarly, heaven is a place of unity and nearness. Earth is broken into discord. Separation is the law of earth. But there are no distances in heaven. It is called the *"beloved city"* (Rev. 20:9). Affections center there and longings go there in a strong restless current. Beloved of earth and beloved of heaven, the earth's saints have turned their feet to God's home and placed their hearts' dearest love there. Angels hold it in most tender love. Friends are there. In that city they have found their home. Centuries have come and gone since the tired feet of earth's saintly pilgrims found sweet rest and home in that beloved city. None ever go out of that city, for love holds them there.

This city's Maker and Builder is God; *"For he hath prepared for them a city"* (Heb. 11:16). God had much to do with that city. He drew its plans and dug and laid its deep foundations. God built it, God fitted it, God finished it, God lives in it. All life is there direct from God—life in its fullness, vigor, and brightness. God is its Life.

God is its Architect and Contractor; no archangel's matchless taste and incomparable genius were used in drafting the plan of this glorious city. God drew the plan. The inexhaustible stores of God's own wisdom, His divine skill, and His faultless taste brought into perfection the design of the city that was to be the abiding home of His children. God was its Builder. Only He could carry out the original plan. The God who laid the deep foundations of the world and brought into being and order its mighty frame condescended to enter again into the work of creation and built a city as the superb home for His elect ones of earth.

No night darkness rests on this heavenly city. It is emphatically called, *"the city of the living God"* (Heb. 12:22). God is more immediately, more personally, and more gloriously there than anywhere else. Life there has God as its immediate source and supply. This life is in its most opulent fullness, fragrant with all that is sweet, gracious, and attractive and free from all that could in any way affect the perfection of its joy or restrain its endless advance. Glorious God-built city! Who can paint its glories? Who can picture the glories of its blissful inhabitants? It would be a little heaven to see that city and get a sight of its princely citizens.

The New Jerusalem

Heaven is a city protected by jeweled walls. In Bible times, a city was a place where treasure was stored, and its walls kept it safe. Heaven is called the New Jerusalem, not only in opposition to and distinction from the Old Jerusalem, but also to designate its freshness and eternal newness. Never is it to know decay or dullness. It is called the heavenly Jerusalem to distinguish it from the earthly one and also to emphasize its glories.

The earthly Jerusalem was the center of Jewish hopes. Their hearts were there. There was no song, only sadness and exile, when they were away from it. Their hearts were always trembling to that pole, and their prayers were made with windows open toward Jerusalem. All this symbolizes what the heavenly Jerusalem should be to us.

If I forget thee, O Jerusalem, let my right hand forget her cunning. If I do not remember thee, let my tongue cleave to the roof of my mouth; if I prefer not Jerusalem above my chief joy.
(Ps. 137:5–6)

Heaven ought to be far more to us than Jerusalem was to the Jew. *"In this we groan, earnestly desiring to be clothed upon with our house which is from heaven"* (2 Cor. 5:2).

These biblical symbols are designed to draw, stir, and allure, and also to instruct us in the nature of heaven so far as earthly language can convey eternal and heavenly things. The Bible calls heaven a city; this is a familiar biblical symbol of heaven. It is not by accident that this term is a familiar and favorite one. It is suggestive of heaven's manifold nature.

Out of respect for Jewish sanctities and devotion, and as a memorial, heaven was called "The

New Jerusalem." The Jew will find full compensation for the loss of his earthly Jerusalem in this new city, which will endure eternally without decay of luster, renown, or glory.

The term *city* is a familiar type of the heavenly land and heavenly life. A city is the center of power and of life, and heaven is a great city. All the principles and facts that the term *city* brings to mind find their full expression there. The idea of a jeweled and golden city expresses the unsurpassed loveliness and preciousness of that country and its life. The jewels are in the foundations of its walls, and its pavements are made of gold. The most costly materials of earth are used for the lowest and most common uses of heaven, and if its most common and meanest things are jeweled and golden, we have no figures or values to represent the exceeding richness of its higher things. God's capital is a great city, splendid with all the glory of His presence.

Heaven is called a city in reference to the original meaning of the word *city*, which is fullness or throng. Heaven will be full. An innumerable company that no man can number will gather within its walls. Heaven will not be sparsely settled. Its thoroughfares will be crowded; throngs of enraptured feet will press its golden pavements.

The road to heaven is indeed narrow, the gate straight, and few find it. But each community and each generation contributes its few who dare to be singular, who are brave enough to walk and struggle alone. And on through the revolving ages, the few precious ones are being housed in heaven until their number will be great. If you and I miss that happy land, others will shoulder the cross, pass out of the pleasing wide way, and make the solitary journey. They will take the crown that we have so ignobly and foolishly lost.

A city is the symbol of life in its magnificence, perfection, and glory. Heaven will be the realization of all this. Doubtless the closeness of sympathy, love, and fellowship that will abound in heaven are found in this figure of a city.

Living in the Eternal City

The inconstant, passing nature of earth's most substantial and social things is proverbial. Poetry and fiction speak of it. It is part of the sad experience of life, and the most cursory observation confirms our experience that earth is mutable; its fairest flowers fade away, and its most precious joys soon wither. But heaven is enduring. It is not the pilgrim's inn. It is home. It abides, settled forever.

Heaven is a prepared city. It is ready, fitted up, and complete. (See Hebrews 11:16.) Neither untilled soil nor overgrown forests will salute us. Our homes are already built; no strenuous labor faces us. Everything is ready and anticipated, furnished by taste and care, a knowledge and ability that knows all wants, furnishes all comforts, supplies all luxuries, and stops at no expense.

Nothing that stains or is impure can gain an entrance to the holy city. (See Revelation 11:2.) Everything is as brilliant as a diamond, and as pure. It is said to be great in its goodness and light, great in its attractive power, and great in frame, beauty, and grandeur. Everything about the city is most exquisite in charms, most precious in value, and most costly in richness.

The fact that it is a holy city is more important to our purpose and for our good than its greatness. The term *holy* baffles the critics to define it with certainty and clarity. It certainly means separated to God and devoted to Him. It certainly means purity. Earthly cities are great, but their purity is often in an inverse ratio to their greatness. In heaven, greatness is never divorced from goodness. This is, sadly, not so on earth. Heaven is a city whose purity clarifies its atmosphere and causes it to sparkle and glitter like crystal. It is a city whose light is in its purity. Its brightness and permanence emanate from God and the Lamb.

Manifestations of Glory

And there came unto me one of the seven angels which had the seven vials full of the seven last plagues, and talked with me, saying, Come hither, I will show thee the bride, the Lamb's wife. And he carried me away in the spirit to a great and high mountain, and showed me that great city, the holy Jerusalem, descending out of heaven from God, having the glory of God: and her light was like unto a stone most precious, even like a jasper stone, clear as crystal; and had a wall great and high.   (Rev. 21:9–12)

It took the light and power of the Spirit and the perspective elevation and sublimity of a mountaintop to view this city in its inexhaustible magnificence and ever increasing glory. What grandeur in that vision! The ecstasy of spirit and inspiration of the great mountains heightened and made the view ravishing, but these could transfer but a faint resemblance to the reality. It is a picture of exquisite and unfading beauty, but a picture only. The life, the reality, the substance cannot be portrayed by any inspired trance or grand and lofty mountain view.

The glory of God is the highest and the most splendid brightness of His uncreated glory. It is certainly the completed exhibition of highest excellence and supreme beauty. The revelation of God is this glory, and it forms the light, blessedness, and splendor of the city. What a land! What a life! Here the glory of God constitutes the loveliness and glory of the land—the opulence and wealth of its life! Her light is like a stone most precious, God's glory the sun! The light coming from such a sun would dazzle and flame like earth's most costly, beautiful, brilliant, and sparkling diamond.

Surrounded by Strength and Beauty

The walls and the gates find their expressive significance in Isaiah: *"Call thy walls Salvation, and thy gates Praise"* (Isa. 60:18).

Behold, I will lay thy stones with fair colours, and lay thy foundations with sapphires. And I will make thy windows of agates, and thy gates of carbuncles, and all thy borders of pleasant stones. (Isa. 54:11–12)

We have a strong city: *"Salvation will God appoint for walls and bulwarks"* (Isa. 26:1).

The walls represent the strength and power of the salvation of the heavenly life. So evident and mighty are the forces of salvation in heaven that it fills with transporting rapture and goes out with unrestrained, spontaneous, and mighty energy:

After this I beheld, and, lo, a great multitude, which no man could number, of all nations, and kindreds, and people, and tongues, stood before the throne, and before the Lamb, clothed with white robes, and palms in their hands; and cried with a loud voice, saying, Salvation to our God which sitteth upon the throne, and unto the Lamb. And all the angels stood round about the throne, and about the elders and the four beasts, and fell before the throne on their faces, and worshipped God, saying, Amen: blessing, and glory, and wisdom, and thanksgiving, and honour, and power, and might, be unto our God for ever and ever. Amen. (Rev. 7:9–12)

The hope of salvation ought to be joyous, glorious, and hope-inspiring to us on earth. But as much as it is to us, it is much more to them in heaven. We have the brook, they have ocean streams; we have the glitter and mildness of starlight, they have the sun in its unclouded strength.

The wall is great and high:

And the wall of the city had twelve foundations,
and in them the names of the twelve apostles of
the Lamb....And the building of the wall of it was
of jasper: and the city was pure gold, like unto
clear glass. And the foundations of the wall of the
city were garnished with all manner of precious
stones.   (Rev. 21:14, 18–19)

The walls are for protection. The twelve foundations indicate strength, while the jewels represent the beauty and preciousness of this strength. The heavenly life will be a protected life, walled in by massive strength and jeweled beauty, to adorn and enrich. We will be held in heaven. We will go out no more. The motives and influences that hold us to heaven will be strong, but not like iron—dull, heavy, and strong. The walls are jasper, and all the twelve foundations are jeweled with every variety of precious stone.

The forces binding us to heaven will not imprison us, but will hold us there by forces as strong as walls of iron, and as resplendent as jasper—as strong as twelve foundations can make them, but as rich, as various, as brightly glorious, as the jewels with which they are emblazoned.

The building material of the walls of the city was jasper. We have in the third chapter this description of God: *"And immediately I was in the spirit; and, behold, a throne was set in heaven, and one sat on the throne. And he that sat was to look upon like a jasper and a sardine stone"* (Rev. 4:2–3).

How remarkable are the walls of the heavenly city, made out of the same material! How closely God and His city are allied and unified, when this same book says:

> *Him that overcometh will I make a pillar in the temple of my God, and he shall go no more out: and I will write upon him the name of my God, and the name of the city of my God, which is new Jerusalem, which cometh down out of heaven from my God: and I will write upon him my new name.* (Rev. 3:12)

The city was pure gold, transparent, and reflecting every form of beauty, far surpassing in richness, purity, and value any earthly gold.

All figures and values are exhausted in the description. No earthly values of wealth and loveliness can exceed these! Earthly vocabularies are exhausted, yet only the outside is described. What there is of wealth and good inside defies all language to convey, all beauty to describe. Diamonds, gold, and jewels are valueless compared to that glorious city, its life and its purified beings, and the employments and engagements inside those gates of pearl and walls of jasper.

All these outward adornments, so unparalleled in their value and preciousness, are indicative in their richness and rareness of the principal joys and pursuits of the heavenly life. How godlike are the persons whose stable and precious characters are represented by jeweled foundations! It is a glorious land whose light and purity glitter like brilliant diamonds, whose society is as flawless and pure as transparent gold.

"Thy gates Praise" (Isa. 60:18)—the gates are places of council, wisdom, adornment, and power. The gates are of one pearl each. There are twelve of them, of unrivaled beauty, cost, and purity. They are entrances and impress us with the unity, purity, and worth of all who enter there. Those holy gates forever bar pollution, sin, and shame. The angels have much to do with the entrance into the heavenly gates and much to do with the stay there. All that is termed kingly, all that belongs to honor and glory, are in that heavenly city.

The very pavement, trodden under foot, lowly and dishonored, is made of earth's purest gold and mirrors the forms of heavenly saints who walk along its streets. Their forms are too beautiful to rest their shadows on any substance less precious than gold refined and polished to its highest perfection. And those forms are too beautiful not to be reflected and constantly mirrored as they pass along. These forms and images of perfect beauty add much to the charms of the city.

In this world, death reigns. There, life reigns:

And he showed me a pure river of water of life, clear as crystal, proceeding out of the throne of God and of the Lamb. In the midst of the street of it, and on either side of the river, was there the tree of life, which bare twelve manner of fruits, and yielded her fruit every month: and the leaves of the tree were for the healing of the nations. And there shall be no more curse: but the throne of God and of the Lamb shall be in it; and his servants shall serve him. (Rev. 22:1–3)

Heaven will be life in its full vigor, like a river, deep and exhaustless and wide. A river it will be—not a branch, nor a well, but a river, ever expanding and ever moving on. All things in heaven will be to refresh, to gladden, and to give and increase life. A powerful river, heaven's life flows out of the throne of God. God's throne is the symbol of God's rule and God's power.

The Lamb That Was Slain

Heaven will be the place where God's power will be seen and felt. He will rule with unlimited power and absolute authority, but the issuance will be the *"river of water of life, clear as crystal"* (v. 1). We are constantly reminded that heaven is all purity. Its life is a river, fully charged and strong in current, but transparent, crystalline in its purity.

The throne is not separate from the Lamb. The Son of God and His atoning sacrifice unite with the throne to enrich the current of the heavenly life. In the heavenly world, through all its happy life, as the source of its most entrancing vision and the school of its profoundest lessons, it will always and everywhere and in everything be *"a Lamb as it had been slain"* (Rev. 5:6). Forever will the melody of heaven go on:

And they sung a new song, saying, Thou art worthy to take the book, and to open the seals thereof: for thou wast slain, and hast redeemed us to God by thy blood out of every kindred, and tongue, and people, and nation; and hast made us unto our God kings and priests: and we shall reign on the earth. And I beheld, and I heard the voice of many angels round about the throne and the beasts and the elders: and the number of them was ten thousand times ten thousand, and thousands of thousands; saying with a loud voice, Worthy is the Lamb that was slain to receive power, and riches, and wisdom, and strength, and honour, and glory, and blessing.
(Rev. 5:9–12)

Every new avenue of delight, every new discovery in the heavenly life, will be the unfolding of the wonderful mystery, unlimited glories, and exhaustless power of *"the Lamb slain from the foundation of the world"* (Rev. 13:8), the Christ crucified, as well as the enthroned God. Everything in heaven will combine to further the vigor, expansion, and glory of that life. The Tree of Life will continually produce its fruit with the freshness, frequency, and energy of monthly crops. Its very leaves are health-giving and invigorating.

The curse, with its withering and deadening disease, and all the dire effects of Adam's fall will be removed. No traces of the first man's steps will be seen or felt. The cause of earth's groaning and sighing will be destroyed. But the power of God—with all its benign and recreating energy and the power of the Cross to redeem, renew, and perfect—will be.

Perfected in Truth

Service of the highest, most adoring, and enrapturing form will characterize heaven. All will be melody and praise, without a discordant note.

The inhabitants of heaven will have a perfect vision of God. That vision will be the melody, study, and pursuit of glorified spirits. To know God, and to know more of Him, will be the employment and bliss of heaven. Believers will be sealed for Him with His name in their foreheads. The sign of ownership, the distinctive mark of loyalty and consecration to God—without the hands of church or priest, of sacrament or ceremony, rite or ritual—will be placed on them. They come to Him in person, and from Him they receive directly all His treasure for each passing moment of the eternal life.

In heaven, all lesser lights are obscured, and all intermediaries retired. God and Christ, with all the fullness of their divine and eternal affluence, are in constant, personal contact. The light of God's presence hides and disperses all the feeble lights of earth. God shines with splendor on the glorified ones, and all the divine authority of the Cross lifts them to royal privileges. They are not only priests but kings to God. Earth has no insight into the exalted glories its inhabitants will be lifted to in heaven. It has no concept of the grandeur to which they will be exalted and no thought or imagination of the scepter that will be put into the hands of the heirs when their inheritance is received.

Does the vision of John transport and delight us? Then heaven is the place where our thirstings for Him are satisfied and our visions of Him are perfect, glorious, and indescribable.

With sublime and soothing truth, the Bible continually declares the superiority of the heavenly life. Heaven robes the saints and transports them with a deathless and painless life. Its length is eternal and its conditions are absolute. There is eternal freedom from every form of evil, and there is the presence of every form of good and greatness. How glorious is this when its truth possesses us and lifts us above the earthly life with its relative littleness and its unmeasurable ills! The heavenly home—a crown of glory—is an unspeakable joy!

> *And there shall be no more curse: but the throne of God and of the Lamb shall be in it; and his servants shall serve him: and they shall see his face; and his name shall be in their foreheads. And there shall be no night there; and they need no candle, neither light of the sun; for the Lord God giveth them light: and they shall reign for ever and ever.* (Rev. 22:3–5)

There are difficulties in interpreting John's revelation. The diversities and antagonisms of construction are almost endless. But to whatever school of interpretation the truth may attach, one thing is sure: The description of the heavenly Jerusalem in its last chapters is the pattern after which the earthly is to be shaped.

As Moses' tabernacle was the pattern of the heavenly, so the literal, real heaven—the heaven of fact and place, the third heaven where God abides and is seen in His unveiled glory—is photographed by John and presented as the model and final result of God's work on earth. The tabernacle was only shown to Moses on the Mount, but the pattern of it was shaped by the original in heaven, and the Jew who studied and followed the pattern understood the principles and substance of the original. We study this picture of the heavenly to know what heaven is.

To that Jerusalem above
With singing I repair;
While in the flesh, my hope and love,
My heart and soul, are there:
There my exalted Savior stands,
My merciful High Priest,
And still extends His wounded hands,
To take me to His breast.

—Charles Wesley

3

Heaven: a Kingdom, a Crown, an Inheritance

HAPPY WILL I BE AND FOREVER HAPPY, IF AFTER DEATH I MIGHT HEAR THE MELODY OF THOSE HYMNS AND HALLELUJAHS WHICH THE CITIZENS OF THAT CELESTIAL KINGDOM AND THE SQUADRON OF THOSE BLESSED SPIRITS SING IN PRAISE OF THE ETERNAL KING. THIS IS THAT SWEET MUSIC WHICH ST. JOHN HEARD IN THE REVELATION, WHEN THE INHABITANTS OF HEAVEN SANG, "LET ALL THE WORLD BLESS THEE, O LORD." TO THEE BE GIVEN ALL HONOR AND DOMINION FOR A WORLD OF WORLDS. AMEN.
—JEREMY TAYLOR

A Kingdom

What magnificence and splendor there are in a kingdom! What ambitions result from the desire to possess a kingdom! It is a stimulant to noblest effort. Heaven is to be won as a kingdom is won. Heaven is to be struggled for as a kingdom is struggled for. Heaven stimulates as a kingdom stimulates.

The work of grace in the human heart is called a kingdom, the kingdom of grace. Heaven is called a kingdom, the kingdom of glory. *"Come, ye blessed of my Father, inherit the kingdom prepared for you"* (Matt. 25:34) are Jesus' words as He rewards the honored ones who are on His right hand in the Day of Judgment.

Peter warned, *"That ye would walk worthy of God, who hath called you unto his kingdom and glory"* (1 Thess. 2:12). Here we have a combination of kingdom and glory. What a magnificent combination! James said, *"Rich in faith, and heirs of the kingdom"* (James 2:5). Peter declared, *"An entrance shall be ministered unto you abundantly into the everlasting kingdom of our Lord and Saviour Jesus Christ"* (2 Peter 1:11).

The future life is declared to be a throne: *"To him that overcometh will I grant to sit with me in my throne, even as I also overcame, and am set down with my Father in his throne"* (Rev. 3:21).

A Crown

It is a crown: *"Hold that fast which thou hast, that no man take thy crown"* (Rev. 3:11). It is an incorruptible crown, a crown whose glory never dims, whose power never abates. Paul spoke of the Isthmian games and their runners, their strenuous self-denial and arduous efforts: *"Now they do it to obtain a corruptible crown; but we an incorruptible"* (1 Cor. 9:25).

Paul declared at the very point of death:

> *Henceforth there is laid up for me a crown of righteousness, which the Lord, the righteous judge, shall give me at that day: and not to me only, but unto all them also that love his appearing.* (2 Tim. 4:8)

"A crown of righteousness," awarded according to rigid demands of integrity. *"A crown of life"* (Rev. 2:10)! James said,

> *Blessed is the man that endureth temptation: for when he is tried, he shall receive the crown of life, which the Lord hath promised to them that love him.* (James 1:12)

Peter declared, *"And when the chief Shepherd shall appear, ye shall receive a crown of glory that fadeth not away"* (1 Peter 5:4). How this stimulates us to the strictest temperance and self-denial!

> *Know ye not that they which run in a race run all, but one receiveth the prize? So run, that ye may obtain. And every man that striveth for the mastery is temperate in all things. Now they do it to obtain a corruptible crown; but we an incorruptible. I therefore so run, not as uncertainly; so fight I, not as one that beateth the air: but I keep under my body, and bring it into subjection: lest that by any means, when I have preached to others, I myself should be a castaway.* (1 Cor. 9:24–27)

This was the effect of this incorruptible crown on the chief of the apostles.

How grand the awards of eternity are! A kingdom, authority, elevation, and grandeur are in it! A crown belongs to kingly heads, to conquerors, and to heroes. Kingship belongs to it. Overcomers and conquerors enter the realms of life. Grecian athletes were stimulated to amazing feats by a perishable crown. In order to win these perishable crowns, there were no toils they would not endure nor efforts they would not put forth. The spectators of their race, the judge, and the crown are all presented as examples for us in our race for heaven.

Our Inheritance

In Revelation, we have a sweeping declaration of heirship: *"He that overcometh shall inherit all things; and I will be his God, and he shall be my son"* (Rev. 21:7).

In Colossians, we have a combination of reward and inheritance: *"Knowing that of the Lord ye shall receive the reward of the inheritance: for ye serve the Lord Christ"* (Col. 3:24).

Heaven is called an inheritance. It comes by relationship and heirship:

> *For ye have not received the spirit of bondage again to fear; but ye have received the Spirit of adoption, whereby we cry, Abba, Father. The Spirit itself beareth witness with our spirit, that we are the children of God: and if children, then heirs; heirs of God, and joint-heirs with Christ; if*

so be that we suffer with him, that we may be also glorified together. (Rom. 8:15–17)

And in Galatians 4:6–7, we read,

And because ye are sons, God hath sent forth the Spirit of his Son into your hearts, crying, Abba, Father. Wherefore thou art no more a servant, but a son; and if a son, then an heir of God through Christ.

Peter had a magnificent statement of the heirship and the future inheritance of the saints in heaven:

Blessed be the God and Father of our Lord Jesus Christ, which according to his abundant mercy hath begotten us again unto a lively hope by the resurrection of Jesus Christ from the dead, to an inheritance incorruptible, and undefiled, and that fadeth not away, reserved in heaven for you, who are kept by the power of God through faith unto salvation. (1 Peter 1:3–5)

It is represented as a gift: *"The gift of God is eternal life"* (Rom. 6:23).

These rich and diverse expressions depict heaven as a great *reward,* a magnificent and imperishable inheritance of fadeless beauty and unending richness; a *prize,* the greatest of time or eternity; a *gift,* unspeakable and indescribable in all its elements. Heaven's inspiration has produced the saintliest saints, the most heroic heroes, the greatest conquerors, and the most self-denying servants.

How strong are the stimulating forces that heaven awakens! When they are held in our minds and hearts as they ought to be held, in deepest conviction, in most ardent faith, and in interested loyalty, we cannot dispense with them. These heavenly forces are always strengthening our weariness, elevating our depression, and brightening our darkness. They are always calling us to purity and nobleness, always charging us to awaken to righteousness and cease sinning.

The mighty quickener of faith is heaven. The only sure and solid foundation of hope is heaven. The only solution of earth's mysteries, the only righter of earth's wrongs, the only cure for worldliness, is heaven. We need an infusion of heaven into our faith and hope that will create a homesickness for that blessed place. God's home is heaven. Eternal life and all good were born there and flourish there. All life, all happiness, all beauty, all glory, are native to the home of God.

And all this belongs to and awaits the heirs of God in heaven. What a glorious inheritance! What a pleasing prospect!

'Tis God's all-animating voice
That calls thee from on high;
'Tis His own hand presents the prize
To thine aspiring eye —

That prize, with peerless glories bright,
Which shall new luster boast,

When victors' wreaths and monarchs' gems
Shall blend in common dust.

Blest Savior, introduced by Thee,
Have I my race begun;
And, crowned with victory, at Thy feet
I'll lay my honors down

—Philip Doddridge

4

Paradise and Eternal Life

GO ON, AND FAINT NOT. SOMETHING OF YOURS IS IN HEAVEN, BESIDE THE FLESH OF YOUR EXALTED SAVIOR; AND YE GO ON AFTER YOUR OWN. TIME'S THREAD IS SHORTER BY AN INCH THAN IT WAS. AN OATH IS SWORN AND PAST THE SEALS; WHETHER AFFLICTIONS WILL OR WILL NOT, YE MUST GROW, AND SWELL OUT OF YOUR SHELL, AND LIVE, AND TRIUMPH AND REIGN, AND BE MORE THAN A CONQUEROR. FOR YOUR CAPTAIN WHO LEADETH YOU ON IS MORE THAN CONQUEROR AND HE MAKETH YOU PARTAKER OF HIS CONQUEST AND VICTORY.

—SAMUEL RUTHERFORD

P aul used the word *paradise* as equivalent to the third heaven—the abode of God. (See 2 Corinthians 12:2.) The word *paradise* is also used in Revelation, *"To him that overcometh will I give to eat of the tree of life, which is in the midst of the paradise of God"* (Rev. 2:7).

Paradise is a separated and distinguished place. It is emphasized as a marked and distinct place, and as a place of eminent distinction and beauty. It is the abode of God and angelic beings where true Christians will be taken after death.

God's paradise—how matchless its beauty! How unparalleled in every excellence, dignity, and loveliness it must be! The thief was to be translated to that gracious home *the same day* the jeering and infuriated mob crucified him with Jesus in order that his cross might defame that of the Son of God. But instead of increasing the ignominy and shame of Jesus, it added to the luster and power of that Cross by lifting a robber from the shame and guilt of the cross to the glorious beauties of heaven! *"To day shalt thou be with me in paradise"* (Luke 23:43) has given hope of immortality to many a sinner as he has lifted his prayerful, dying eyes and said, *"Remember me"* (v. 42).

Heaven is a place of rarest beauty and purity, and yet sinful robbers go there, washed in the blood of the Lamb. *"With me"*—what exalted glory, supreme dignity, and divine companionship for a thief! How close the union, how infinite the condescension of Jesus, to be his companion and to share His glory and joy with him!

One of the noblest memorials to the death of Jesus is that thief lifted from the cross of guilt to a throne of glory. The wonders of that death! What tongue can tell of its marvels? What imagination can discover its miracles? *"To day shalt thou be with me in paradise"* is only the beginning.

Resurrected to Life

In His notable conversation with Nicodemus, Jesus explained that the position to which He will elevate believers is *"eternal life."*

> *And as Moses lifted up the serpent in the wilderness, even so must the Son of man be lifted up: that whosoever believeth in him should not perish, but have eternal life. For God so loved the world, that he gave his only begotten Son, that whosoever believeth in him should not perish, but have everlasting life.* (John 3:14–16)

Again, in the fourth chapter, the eternal glory is designated as eternal life; it is the harvest of our faithful sowing and tilling in this life.

> *And he that reapeth receiveth wages, and gathereth fruit unto life eternal: that both he that soweth and he that reapeth may rejoice together.* (John 4:36)

The resurrection is *"unto life."*

> *Marvel not at this: for the hour is coming, in the which all that are in the graves shall hear his voice, and shall come forth; they that have done good, unto the resurrection of life; and they that have done evil, unto the resurrection of damnation.* (John 5:28–29)

Jesus' wonderful words to Martha declare the great truth that the crowning glory of the future is eternal life:

> *Jesus saith unto her, Thy brother shall rise again. Martha saith unto him, I know that he shall rise again in the resurrection at the last day. Jesus said unto her, I am the resurrection, and the life: he that believeth in me, though he were dead, yet shall he live: and whosoever liveth and believeth in me shall never die. Believest thou this? She saith unto him, Yea, Lord: I believe that thou art the Christ, the Son of God, which should come into the world.* (John 11:23–27)

Jesus also said, *"He that loveth his life shall lose it; and he that hateth his life in this world shall keep it unto life eternal"* (John 12:25).

Jesus gave His disciples a magnificent, comforting promise before His death, while the gloom of Gethsemane and Calvary was on them and on Him:

> *Let not your heart be troubled: ye believe in God, believe also in me. In my Father's house are many mansions: if it were not so, I would have told you. I go to prepare a place for you. And if I go and prepare a place for you, I will come again, and receive you unto myself; that where I am, there ye may be also.* (John 14:1–3)

Heaven will relieve all the troubles of this life. Every earthly pain is to be eased, all fiery trials quenched, all tears dried by heaven.

Dwelling in His Presence

In God's house of many mansions, Jesus holds sway, sits upon His throne, and manifests His glory. There, with their exalted Lord, His saints dwell in eternal, unalloyed good. We see not only the purpose and inflexible decree of Jesus to have us in His Father's house, but also the longings of His heart: *"Where I am, there ye may be also"* (John 14:3).

This comes out most fully in His high priestly prayer:

> *Father, I will that they also, whom thou hast given me, be with me where I am; that they may behold my glory, which thou hast given me.*
> (John 17:24)

We will not be idle spectators of that glory, but we will share in it as well as see it. That Jesus wants us with Him is not a mere sentiment to adorn or sweeten but a declared, operative, and eternal decree: *"Father, I will."* His heart and authority are in it.

"Having a desire to depart, and to be with Christ; which is far better," Paul said in Philippians 1:23. To be in heaven is to be with Christ.

That Jesus has gone to heaven *"to appear in the presence of God for us"* (Heb. 9:24) is true. By the mystery and ministry of His death and the glory of His intercession, He is preparing a place for us and preparing us for the place.

Jesus is exalted in heaven at the right hand of the throne of God. The throne is a symbol of power, and the right hand is a symbol of honor, glory, and majesty. Jesus is exalted to the highest place in heaven to which God's power can raise Him. The apostle declared the exalted dignity of Jesus thus:

According to the working of his mighty power, which he wrought in Christ, when he raised him from the dead, and set him at his own right hand in the heavenly places, far above all principality, and power, and might, and dominion, and every name that is named, not only in this world, but also in that which is to come: and hath put all things under his feet, and gave him to be the head over all things to the church, which is his body, the fulness of him that filleth all in all.
(Eph. 1:19-23)

The highest position of legal glory is His, and we are to be partners with Him in all the splendors and advantages of the eternal world. God crowns, exalts, and glorifies Jesus with such divine magnificence! With the same exhaustless magnificence the Son dispenses the boundless wealth of heaven to His glorified ones.

What Jesus has done for us here in His startling advent and His unparalleled humiliation and suffering is a mirror of the wonderful, unspeakable, and indescribable things that He will do for us in the other world. But it is only a faint reflection of them. For His ability is greater, and the conditions far more favorable, in heaven than when under the limitations that restricted Him here.

What the material blessings and settings of that heavenly life will be, we cannot tell. But we may be well assured that they will be of the purest and most exquisite form and material.

Of one thing we are constantly reminded: that Jesus will be with us and will serve us, like a shepherd feeding his flock, on the richest and best food of heaven. He will lead us to new and living fountains of bliss, knowledge, and light. To have Jesus with us will be the sum of all happiness, of all perfection, of all good. What beauty there is in His face! What wealth untold in His character! Only eternity can tell His unlimited resources to bless.

Christ has matchless, indescribable charms for those who are possessed by His love. While in prison, the gifted and saintly Samuel Rutherford used his great gifts, which by his great love are turned to poetry, to speak of Jesus and His loveliness:

> I never believed till now that there was so much to be found in Christ on this side death and heaven. Oh, the ravishments of heavenly joy which may be had here, in the small gleanings and comforts that fall from Christ.

If Jesus was so much to the gifted and holy Samuel Rutherford, while he was banished and a prisoner and in this world, what must He be to those in heaven? We cannot fathom what indescribable beauties are in the unfoldings of His character to the glorified. What a heaven it must be!

It cannot be said too strongly that we are bound to love heaven for Jesus' sake. We are bound to long for heaven because Jesus is there. We are bound to be filled joy when the hour comes to go there because it is the hour to see Jesus, the hour to meet Jesus, the hour to enjoy Jesus, and to enjoy Him forever.

O Paradise, O Paradise,
Who doth not crave for rest?
Who would not seek the happy land
Where they that loved are blest;

Where loyal hearts and true,
Stand ever in the light,
All rapture, through and through
In God's most holy sight?

O Paradise! O Paradise!
The world is growing old;
Who would not be at rest and free
Where love is never cold?

5

A Truer Life

After it was noised about that Mr. Valiant-for-truth was taken with a summons by the same post as the other, and had this for a token that the summons was true, that "his pitcher was broken at the fountain." When he understood it he called for his friends and told them of it. Then said he, "I am going to my Father's and though with great difficulty I got hither yet now I do not repent me of all the trouble I have been at to arrive where I am." When the day that he must go over was come many accompanied him to the river-side, into which as he went he said, "Death, where is thy sting? Grave, where is thy victory?" So he passed over, and all the trumpets sounded for him on the other side.
—John Bunyan

The Bible often uses the term *life* as the central and fundamental idea of heaven—its enjoyments, employments, and character.

The term is almost too literal to be reckoned as a symbol. It is a comprehensive symbol, and its nearness to the literal enhances its value as a symbol.

The New Testament abounds in the use of this symbol. It is the sum and result of the Gospel. Faith plants the seed of eternal life, and it grows in the faithful heart through all the struggles and years of this life. But it finds its eternal unfolding in fullest expansion and amplitude in heaven. *"As many as were ordained to eternal life"* (Acts 13:48).

> *To them who by patient continuance in well doing seek for glory and honour and immortality, eternal life.* (Rom. 2:7)

> *That as sin hath reigned unto death, even so might grace reign through righteousness unto eternal life by Jesus Christ our Lord.* (Rom. 5:21)

To "reign in life" means this:

> *But now being made free from sin, and become servants to God, ye have your fruit unto holiness, and the end everlasting life. For the wages of sin is death; but the gift of God is eternal life through Jesus Christ our Lord.* (Rom. 6:22–23)

Desiring Full Life

In giving the reason why the true Christian groans to enter into heaven, Paul said,

> *For we that are in this tabernacle do groan, being burdened: not for that we would be unclothed, but*

clothed upon, that mortality might be swallowed up of life.   (2 Cor. 5:4)

To Timothy, Paul said, *"Lay hold on eternal life, whereunto thou art also called"* (1 Tim. 6:12). He exhorted the rich in this way:

That they do good, that they be rich in good works, ready to distribute, willing to communicate; laying up in store for themselves a good foundation against the time to come, that they may lay hold on eternal life.   (1 Tim. 6:18–19)

James designated heaven as a *"crown of life"* (James 1:12). It was called *"the resurrection of life"* (John 5:29). The statements of the apostles and Christ that use this symbol of heavenly life imply that it is an eternal freedom from and opposition to death. Every good that man can desire to enjoy is concentrated in the term *life*. Heaven is the possession of the first and last blessing of man. It is the essence of all happiness. Life is the state and affluence of heaven—immortal and undecayed with no liability to decay or diminish. The state, environments, and advances of the heavenly world are all life, more life—deeper, wider, sweeter life. Its book is the Book of Life; its river, the River of Life; its tree, the Tree of Life; its water, the Water of Life.

Life was the all engrossing question of the young man who came to Jesus and asked, *"What shall I do that I may inherit eternal life?"* (Mark 10:17).

How attractive and charmful this life is! This life is a divine gift! It is bounded by the cradle, the symbol of helplessness and want, and by death, the impersonation of all that is dark, painful, and terrific. We are enfeebled by disease, hampered by sickness, and marred by severe struggles and sad disappointments. Yet we cling to it and surrender it only in a despairing or triumphant struggle.

But eternal life involves the untold, unimagined, and fadeless glories of heaven! What measureless wealth! What deathless raptures! What glorious intoxication! No description dare attempt its picture. The most exalted strains of music would be discord to the harmony of heaven, and the brightest vision would turn to darkest midnight! All summer suns would chill like the ice of December when contrasted with the splendor of heaven's nightless day. The most gifted, exalted, and sweetest poetry of earth would be but dull prose in heaven.

What is eternal life? Who can dream or imagine that life? Heaven has it! Heaven holds it! It will be the surprise of the saints as they leave earth and pass through the gates of the Celestial City.

Jesus will lead the heavenly inhabitants to *"living fountains of waters"* (Rev. 7:17). In this we have the figure of life, ever new and continuous. Here is a life that refreshes, blesses, and satisfies the soul as water refreshes, blesses, and satisfies the body. Here is a constant unfolding of life full and overflowing like a fountain. Here are new discoveries of life, its hidden sources having been opened up.

Heaven will be the pursuit of life, the employment of life, the enjoyment of life, and the increase of life. Its pursuits, its employment, and its enjoyment will be eternal. Life in heaven will be a rapture, a bliss untold. All the man—mind, soul, and spirit—will be widened and elevated, deepened, refined, and beautified by it. Everything will conspire to make that life supremely blessed and supremely glorious. Christ will feed that life in the richest pastures and lead us to fountains of living water. *"God shall wipe away all tears"* (Rev. 7:17, 21:4) from the eyes of that life.

The heavens shall glow with splendor,
But brighter far than they
The saints shall shine in glory,
As Christ shall them array:
The beauty of the Savior,
Shall dazzle every eye,
In the crowning day that's coming by and by.
Our pain shall then be over,
We'll sin and sigh no more;
Behind us all of sorrow,
And naught but joy before,
A joy in our Redeemer,
As we to Him are nigh,
In the crowning day that's coming by and by.

6

A Foretaste and a Pledge

*THE EYE OF FLESH IS NOT CAPABLE OF SEEING,
NOR THE EAR OF HEARING, NOR THE HEART OF
UNDERSTANDING HEAVEN AND ITS GLORIES. BUT
THERE THE EYE, THE EAR, AND THE HEART ARE MADE
CAPABLE. ELSE HOW COULD WE ENJOY THOSE THINGS
IN HEAVEN? THE MORE PERFECT THE SIGHT, THE
MORE DELIGHTFUL WILL BE THE BEAUTIFUL OBJECT.
THE MORE PERFECT THE APPETITE, THE SWEETER
THE FOOD; THE MORE MUSICAL THE EAR, THE MORE
PLEASANT THE MELODY; AND THE MORE PERFECT THE
SOUL, THE MORE JOYOUS THESE JOYS, AND THE MORE
GLORIOUS THESE GLORIES.*   —RICHARD BAXTER

The Holy Spirit in us is said to be the "earnest of heaven." The *earnest* is the security and foretaste, and so the Holy Spirit is the certainty of heaven. He puts the fact, taste, power, and the ambition and toil for heaven freshly, strongly, and constantly in our hearts. The refrain and chorus He teaches us is, "Heaven is my home."

> *In whom ye also trusted, after that ye heard the word of truth, the gospel of your salvation: in whom also after that ye believed, ye were sealed with that holy Spirit of promise, which is the earnest of our inheritance until the redemption of the purchased possession, unto the praise of his glory.*
> (Eph. 1:13–14)

> *Now he which stablisheth us with you in Christ, and hath anointed us, is God; who hath also sealed us, and given the earnest of the Spirit in our hearts.* (2 Cor. 1:21–22)

These great texts present to us the ministry and work of the Holy Spirit as He forms in us the fact and experience of heaven. He shapes us in desire and in heavenliness, in heavenly longings and heavenly fashion at every point.

The music and hope of heaven would fill and sweeten our lives if we lived in the full power of the Spirit. What transporting anticipations! What *"joy unspeakable and full of glory"* (1 Peter 1:8) would brighten our living and dying days! The Spirit's power settles our faith and quickens our sentiments of heaven. By the Spirit's mighty workings, heaven becomes an assured, sublime, and glorious fact.

The power of the Holy Spirit puts us on track toward the good world. He puts a thirst for heaven in us. He gives us constant tastes and visions of heaven, until all other tastes pall and all other visions are heavy and dull. He gives us notes of heaven's harmony and all earth's notes are discord. The power of the Spirit binds us to heaven because Jesus is there. We are bound to love it, think about it, and desire it, for Jesus is its center and glory.

Strongly and insistently, the Holy Spirit uses heaven and its untold, manifold good to move saints to action, awaken them from death, and to increase their zeal and love. The Holy Spirit implants heaven in us. The Holy Spirit Himself, given to us, is God's mark of ownership and security. His authority is put on us.

But it is not His sealing process—its condition, significance, or results in full—that we now consider but the *earnest* of future and eternal things. The Holy Spirit is the earnest of heaven to us. *Earnest* refers to a pledge that a contract will be faithfully and fully carried out. An earnest is part of the thing itself, given as a security that the whole will be given in its time. Through the Holy Spirit, God gives us a part of heaven as a pledge of the full heaven when the time is ripe. The Holy Spirit is to us both a foretaste and a pledge of heaven.

The Holy Spirit puts heaven in us when He dwells in us. All our tastes, struggles, desires, and longings for heaven are the creations of His power and the sure tests of His presence. If there is no heavenly spirit and no heavenly yearnings in us, there is no Holy Spirit in us. God fits us for the heavenly world by the Holy Spirit and plants in us the heavenly mind and image. The indwelling Spirit of God makes us less like earth and more like heaven. The Holy Spirit matures hope to its brightest luster and enables the saint to *"glory in tribulations"* (Rom. 5:3) and *"rejoice in hope of the glory of God"* (v. 2).

Pressing on toward Heaven

Paul, by the spirit, promoted heaven. In mid-career, fastened to life and earth by his strenuous toil, Paul paused to record his loyalty to heaven and to Jesus; for, in Paul's estimation, and in every true estimation, they are one. *"I am in a strait betwixt two, having a desire to depart, and to be with Christ; which is far better"* (Phil. 1:23).

We find him on the stretch bound for heaven, always *"confident...and willing rather to be absent from the body, and to be present with the Lord"* (2 Cor. 5:8). He was ever pressing on:

> *Forgetting those things which are behind, and reaching forth unto those things which are before, I press toward the mark for the prize of the high calling of God in Christ Jesus.* (Phil. 3:13–14)

He always kept his body in subjection that he might not lose the incorruptible crown. (See 1 Corinthians 9:25.) At the close—his good battle fought, his course finished, the faith kept—heaven was still in full view, its crown gleaming brighter under Nero's axe.

It is the thought, the hope, the fact of heaven that forms Christian character and matures it into its unearthly beauty and perfection.

The stringent demands of entering into eternal life could not be set forth more acutely or with more terrific colorings than by Jesus Christ:

> *If thy hand offend thee, cut it off: it is better for thee to enter into life maimed, than having two hands to go into hell, into the fire that never shall be quenched.* (Mark 9:43)

Heaven is termed a reward. *"Great is your reward in heaven"* (Matt. 5:12), Christ said to His persecuted and reviled disciples. And so it says in Revelation: *"And, behold, I come quickly; and my reward is with me, to give every man according as his work shall be"* (Rev. 22:12). The meaning of *reward* is dues paid for work. *"For the Son of man shall come in the glory of his Father with his angels; and then he shall reward every man according to his works"* (Matt. 16:27).

> *Then let the wildest storms arise;*
> *Let tempests mingle earth and skies;*
> *No fatal shipwrecks shall I fear,*
> *But all my treasures with me bear.*
>
> *If thou, my Jesus, still be nigh,*
> *Cheerful I live, and joyful die;*
> *Secure, when mortal comforts flee,*
> *To find ten thousand worlds in Thee.*

—Philip Doddridge

7

Heaven, a State

AND I HEARD AS IT WERE THE VOICE OF A GREAT MULTITUDE...SAYING, HALLELUJAH: FOR THE LORD OUR GOD, THE ALMIGHTY, REIGNETH. LET US REJOICE AND BE EXCEEDING GLAD...FOR THE MARRIAGE OF THE LAMB IS COME, AND HIS WIFE HATH MADE HERSELF READY. —REVELATION 19:6–7 RV

Heaven is a state as well as a place. Whatever the outward appearance may be, however entrancing to eye, however fascinating to ear, however pleasing to taste or touch, however ecstatic to feeling all the scenes and sounds may be, these are not the prime sources of its attraction. It is a state—a state of enthronement, elevation, and emancipation. It is freedom. Much has been left behind of the old, the worn-out, and the burdensome; and much of the new, the strange, and the wonderful will be there. It will be a state of perfected knowledge. Then we will know even as we are known. God knows us perfectly here. We will know Him and all things perfectly there.

> *For we know in part, and we prophesy in part. But when that which is perfect is come, then that which is in part shall be done away. When I was a child, I spake as a child, I understood as a child, I thought as a child: but when I became a man, I put away childish things. For now we see through a glass, darkly; but then face to face: now I know in part; but then shall I know even as also I am known.* (1 Cor. 13:9–12)

Imagine the unspeakable benefits of a state where we know all things perfectly! There is neither height nor depth nor breadth nor length in heaven, earth, or hell that will not lie open to our knowledge in that exalted and perfected state where all mysteries will be gone.

Freed from Sin, Slave to Christ

In the sixth chapter of Romans, there is a statement vital to heaven: *"But now being made free from sin, and become servants to God, ye have your fruit unto holiness, and the end everlasting life"* (Rom. 6:22). To "make free" is to emancipate. A dual action is seen here—emancipation from sin and enslavement to God. An attitude of repulsion from iniquity, of entire freedom from sin, and an attitude of entire enslavement to God bear the fruit of holiness if found in a heart where God reigns and sin is excluded. Heaven belongs to such a state and character by inheritance, by right.

Two struggles mark the true heavenly life—to be freed from sin and to be wholly devoted to God. How free can I be from sin? How thoroughly devoted to God can I be? These are questions that have engaged and often perplexed the holiest of men. Too much time and thought have been spent by men trying to fix the limits by theoretical statements. The Scriptures make strong affirmations at this point. An elder in Burmah said,

> I find on reading the apostles' writings that they address their fellow Christians and speak of themselves as persons that are dead to sin, buried with Christ into death. They are dead, and their lives are *"hid with Christ in God"* [Col. 3:3]. They have crucified the flesh with its affections and lusts. Their old man is crucified with Christ. They are dead to sin by consequence and are freed from sin. They cease from sin. Being born of God, they sin not; they cannot sin, they have overcome the world, the world is crucified to them and they to the world.
>
> Now these things are mentioned not only as things to be desired or sought after, but as already obtained. *"Ye are dead"* [Col. 3:3], *"have crucified the flesh"* [Gal. 5:24], *"have put off the old man"* [Col. 3:9], are *"freed from sin"* [Rom 6:7], and *"hath ceased from sin"* [1 Peter 4:1].

How many have raised the same questions? Of one thing we may be sure: that the experience and attitude of Christian attainment and obtainment set forth in the New Testament is open to all Christians of every age and every nation. Books on holiness may give us no light and theories may confuse. But with our Bibles before us, the open door of prayer, and the increasing light and power of the Holy Spirit, each of us can settle the question as a personal experience. We must keep this divine statement in our minds: *"Free from sin, and become servants to God"* (Rom. 6:22). This is complete emancipation from sin and enslavement to God, with the full possibilities of God's grace, Christ's blood, the power of the Holy Spirit, and faith.

Set Apart and Sustained

God is *"able to do exceeding abundantly above all that we ask or think"* (Eph. 3:20). *"All things are possible to him that believeth"* (Mark 9:23). *"He that spared not his own Son, but delivered him up for us all, how shall he not with him also freely give us all things?"* (Rom. 8:32).

God has given us all things in Christ that by prayer we can have all that there is in Christ. We are charged to *"be filled with all the fulness of God"* (Eph. 3:19). He is able to make us abound in all grace, that we *"always having all sufficiency in all things, may abound to every good work"* (2 Cor. 9:8). God can *"make you perfect in every good work to do his will, working in you that which is wellpleasing in his sight"* (Heb. 13:21). Then we *"may stand perfect and complete in all the will of God"* (Col. 4:12). All these wonderful Scriptures concerning the possibilities of grace fully answer the question as to how free we can be from sin and how thoroughly we can be devoted to God.

This *"fruit unto holiness"* (Rom. 6:22) is absolutely necessary as a prerequisite for heaven. Without holiness, no one will see the Lord. (See Hebrews 12:14.) Holiness is an imperative, inflexible, eternal condition of heaven. A holy God, a holy Jesus, and a holy heaven demand holiness among men as well as angels.

> *Every man that striveth for the mastery is temperate in all things. Now they do it to obtain a corruptible crown; but we an incorruptible. I therefore so run, not as uncertainly; so fight I, not as one that beateth the air: but I keep under my body, and bring it into subjection: lest that by any means, when I have preached to others, I myself should be a castaway.* (1 Cor. 9:25–27)

The heavenly virtue stressed here is temperance, the strong master of self under the law of strict self-denial. The apostle enforced the necessity of temperance by referring to athletes who spent much time in training, denying themselves things that they enjoyed and that they ordinarily indulged in. Their training, temperance, and strict self-denial were familiar and emphasized this virtue in a strong way.

The apostle was writing of heaven, and the presence of this temperance is not only to be exercised in the higher realms of man's nature but also in the Christian's bodily appetites. Not only is temperance necessary to become a Christian, but its daily and hourly exercise are necessary to continue as a Christian. *"I keep under my body"* means to strike heavily in the face, to render black-and-blue a hard subject, and to reduce it to self-control and bring the body into subjection. The body is the adversary. It is the seat of Satan's temptations, especially that of self-indulgence.

It is through self-control that pride, obstinance, and self-seeking appetites are to be restrained and broken down. The flesh and spirit are to be brought under the law of this heavenly race. No one is free from this law. The apostle declared elsewhere: *"If a man also strive for masteries, yet is he not crowned, except he strive lawfully"* (2 Tim. 2:5). After the race, the winners were examined to see if they had won by lawful means. If they had not, they were deprived of the prize. The law for the heavenly contestants is severe self-control. Without it, all seeming success in the heavenly race will be rejected.

Rejoicing in Redemption

Heaven makes redemption full, the purchase complete, the possession perfect, the pledge sure. Even here we have the foretaste of the full heaven. Heaven is joy unmixed, eternal, and rapturous. Here we have, by the presence of the Holy Spirit, *"joy unspeakable and full of glory"* (1 Peter 1:8). Even here on earth we *"rejoice evermore"* (1 Thess. 5:16).

To rejoice is the command of earth as well as the luxury of heaven.

Heaven is the place and state of perfect rest, but on earth peace reigns through the Holy Spirit. Our peace flows *"as a river"* (Isa. 48:18). *"The peace of God, which passeth all understanding, shall keep your hearts and minds through Christ Jesus"* (Phil. 4:7). This is the type and beginning of heaven's peace. The kingdom of God in this world is *"righteousness, and peace, and joy in the Holy Ghost"* (Rom. 14:17). The kingdom of God in the next world will be but the perfection of righteousness, peace, and joy.

"The redemption of the purchased possession" is changed in the Revised Version to, *"Unto the redemption of God's own possession"* (Eph. 1:14). God's possession of us is by the Holy Spirit, not by redemption. It is not by being bought back only but by God taking possession of us—by yielding ourselves to be filled, possessed, controlled, and owned by God. He is to have unlimited authority over us and supreme, unmixed control in us. That is God's rule here, the precursor and earnest of His reign in heaven. Heaven will give us fullest possession of God, and heaven will give God the fullest possession of us. But heaven is only for those who are God's possession here.

God's Word reveals a land where the misfortune of poverty and the curse of crime never come, where a life of beggary and death on a cross put no stigma on character. Heaven is made up of earth's banished outlaws.

Scripture gives a description of the characters who will be found in heaven:

Others had trial of cruel mockings and scourgings, yea, moreover of bonds and imprisonment: they were stoned, they were sawn asunder, were tempted, were slain with the sword: they wandered about in sheepskins and goatskins; being destitute, afflicted, tormented; (of whom the world was not worthy:) they wandered in deserts, and in mountains, and in dens and caves of the earth.
(Heb. 11:36–38)

Wonderful grace makes saints and immortals of those the earth defamed and ostracized! The beggar Lazarus, and all holy beggars, have learned by their begging the secret of faith. What wonderful companionship and association for our divine Lord—a thief banned by earthly justice to the cross! The power of redemption makes glorious ones of heaven out of the refuse of earth. The Lord has the glorious companionship of a beggar and a robber in paradise! To add to the glory of Himself and to the renown of Abraham, God made Lazarus, earth's ostracized one, His own companion. False estimates, reputations, and rewards of earth are reversed and rectified in Christ's heaven!

In the parable of the rich man and Lazarus, Jesus taught us much of heaven as well as many sad and alarming lessons of hell. All men do not go to heaven. It is possible for all men to go to heaven, but all will not. This we learn from the rich man, who, in hell, lifted up his eyes in torment.

Heaven is not subject to the financial and social influences of this world. Lazarus the beggar had no money, no friends, and no social influence. He had committed the unpardonable crime of earth—that of being a beggar. He was ostracized, friendless, and living without money. He died without friends and was buried without tears. But who can understand heaven? Heaven received Lazarus, the beggar on earth, into more than kingly society; angels became his attendants, and he became the bosom friend and associate of Abraham, the rich man, the *"Friend of God"* (James 2:23). Heavenly society is not based on money nor any of its tributaries, incidents, or accidents. Purity of character reigns in heaven but money does not.

Everlasting Delight

The favorite Bible word used to describe heaven is *glory*, which seems especially suited for it. It means splendor, brightness, magnificence, excellence, preeminence, dignity, majesty in the sense of absolute perfection, an exalted state, and a condition of blessedness.

Heaven will be a happy state. In another place there might be perfection in knowledge and not bliss. There might be progress and pain. There might be glory and splendor that brings no calm to the heart. But heaven's state will be one of supreme, unalloyed happiness, with nothing to shadow its brightness, nothing to bring pain or cause sorrow.

There will be indescribable joy without void, fear, or anxiety.

There are real joys in heaven. We do not understand their fullness, but we know neither listlessness nor weariness will prevail there. Activity is the first and strongest impression we are given of heaven, an activity too intense and profound to be intermittent or joyless. Heaven's joys are of the highest and most engaging order—no fitful delights nor dreamy visions, but joys that fill the heart, mind, and spirit.

We can, perhaps, more readily appreciate heaven's joys by negative statements rather than by positive ones, by the ills we will escape rather than by the joys we will inherit:

No sickness—what an immeasurable bliss! No pain—what endless comfort and ease! No sorrow, no cloud, no night, no weariness, no bitterness, no anguish, no penitence, no remorse, no graves, no sighs, no tears, no sad laments, no broken hearts, no deathbed scenes, no dying there. We will never find a corpse, a coffin, a hearse, or a grave in all that happy, blissful land. No funeral crowd will ever weep, no sorrowing one will ever pass through heaven's streets or walk along its cloudless highways. Not only is there an absence of these things that destroy earth's brightest bliss (and their absence is enough to form a delightful heaven) but there is positive good, *"fulness of joy...pleasures for evermore"* (Ps. 16:11).

No chilling winds, or poisonous breath,
Can reach that healthful shore;
Sickness and sorrow, pain and death,
Are felt and feared no more.

When shall I reach that happy place,
And be forever blest?
When shall I see my Father's face,
And in His bosom rest?

8

Heavenly Virtues

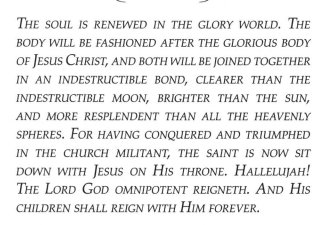

THE SOUL IS RENEWED IN THE GLORY WORLD. THE BODY WILL BE FASHIONED AFTER THE GLORIOUS BODY OF JESUS CHRIST, AND BOTH WILL BE JOINED TOGETHER IN AN INDESTRUCTIBLE BOND, CLEARER THAN THE INDESTRUCTIBLE MOON, BRIGHTER THAN THE SUN, AND MORE RESPLENDENT THAN ALL THE HEAVENLY SPHERES. FOR HAVING CONQUERED AND TRIUMPHED IN THE CHURCH MILITANT, THE SAINT IS NOW SIT DOWN WITH JESUS ON HIS THRONE. HALLELUJAH! THE LORD GOD OMNIPOTENT REIGNETH. AND HIS CHILDREN SHALL REIGN WITH HIM FOREVER.

AN UNHOLY MAN CANNOT ENTER HEAVEN, AND WERE HE IN HEAVEN, IT WOULD BE NO ENJOYMENT TO HIM, BECAUSE IT IS NOT SUITED TO HIM. THE NATURE OF RESIDENT MUST BE SUITED TO THE PLACE OF RESIDENCE....THERE IS A FELLOWSHIP AMONG THE DEVILS IN HELL, AND WITH THOSE WHO ARE OF A DIABOLIC NATURE, AND WE KNOW THAT HOLY INHABITANTS OF HEAVEN ARE BRETHREN WITH HOLY SOULS.
—ADAM CLARKE

Enduring to the End

The results of Paul's argument on the resurrection of the body and its transfiguration for the heavenly world is summarized in this way:

> *Therefore, my beloved brethren, be ye stedfast, unmoveable, always abounding in the work of the Lord, forasmuch as ye know that your labour is not in vain in the Lord.* (1 Cor. 15:58)

"Stedfast" means to be settled, fixed in purpose, not moved, and firmly persistent.

It is said of King Rehoboam, *"He did that which was evil, because he set not his heart to seek the LORD"* (2 Chron. 12:14 RV).

> *He that wavereth is like a wave of the sea driven with the wind and tossed. For let not that man think that he shall receive any thing of the Lord. A double minded man is unstable in all his ways.* (James 1:6–8)

Instability loses heaven. *"My heart is fixed, O God, my heart is fixed"* (Ps. 57:7). That is, the psalmist's heart was seated, settled, and immovable for heaven. No one goes to heaven whose heart is not already there.

Perseverance is a heaven-winning grace. We must be at it always and stay at it all the time. The king of Israel lost his conquest because he struck the ground only three times when he should have struck it twice that many times. (See 2 Kings 13:18–19.) He missed by stopping. We miss heaven by not persevering. Faint-heartedness, weariness, and letting go are fatal conditions in the ascent to heaven. *"And let us not be weary in well doing: for in due season we shall reap, if we faint not"* (Gal. 6:9). It takes strength to gain heaven. They need strong people there. Those who gain heaven are strong. There will be much in this life to create faint-heartedness and much to discourage. To hold on will require resolute fortitude, persevering courage, and steady pushing forward.

Death to Self

The ability to die is a heaven-gaining virtue. Paul said, *"I die daily"* (1 Cor. 15:31). He wanted his dying fashioned after the perfect pattern of Christ: *"Conformable unto his death"* (Phil. 3:10).

> *I am crucified with Christ: nevertheless I live; yet not I, but Christ liveth in me: and the life which I now live in the flesh I live by the faith of the Son of God, who loved me, and gave himself for me.*
> (Gal. 2:20)

Again the apostle said, *"But God forbid that I should glory, save in the cross of our Lord Jesus Christ, by whom the world is crucified unto me, and I unto the world"* (Gal. 6:14).

The cross must be borne along the heavenly way. The cross is the true sign that we are in the heavenly way. As Jesus bore the cross, so must all

His true disciples do the same. As Jesus died on the cross to save us from sin, so must we die to sin, to self, and to the world. It is a painful death, but it is the crowning death. As Jesus went to His Father's right hand from the cross, so we go to His right hand by way of the cross. If there is no shame of the cross, there are no joys of the crown. If there is no death of the cross, there is no life of the crown. If there is no depression of the cross, there is no elevation of the throne.

> *It is a faithful saying: For if we be dead with him, we shall also live with him: if we suffer, we shall also reign with him: if we deny him, he also will deny us.* (2 Tim. 2:11–12)

Building Blocks of Christian Character

In the first chapter of 2 Peter, there is a catalog of the heavenly-fitting graces.

> *And beside this, giving all diligence, add to your faith virtue; and to virtue knowledge; and to knowledge temperance; and to temperance patience; and to patience godliness; and to godliness brotherly kindness; and to brotherly kindness charity.* (vv. 5–7)

The apostle wrote of the wonderful provision God made for our salvation.

> *According as his divine power hath given unto us all things that pertain unto life and godliness, through the knowledge of him that hath called us*

to glory and virtue: whereby are given unto us
exceeding great and precious promises: that by
these ye might be partakers of the divine nature,
having escaped the corruption that is in the world
through lust.   (2 Peter 1:3–4)

In this statement, we have a summary of God's great outlay, laid down before us. We are to contribute, besides what God has done, our quota, or, as the Revised Version says, *"Yea, and for this very cause adding on your part all diligence"* (2 Peter 1:5). In all things concerning heaven, diligence is a necessary virtue. Sustained, persevering, deeply interested effort is a matter of vital importance. Sloth and ease, so criminal and so ensnaring in every department of earthly action and effort, are particularly detrimental in the effort for heaven.

To not be in earnest about heaven is a crime of great magnitude, eternal in fatal consequences. At the very threshold of the path to heaven, we are confronted with the fact that he who wants to win eternal life must be deeply in earnest and express that earnestness by most laborious and persistent effort. Every contestant must bring all diligence to this struggle for heaven at the outset. There can be no slacking of diligence until the heavenly gates are entered. This diligence is put forth to bring to being and perfection all the graces that prepare us for heaven.

"Faith" is the first grace. It is the foundation stone of the whole spiritual building. Faith builds on Jesus Christ.

A foundation will do no good and will be ruined if no house is built on it. The snow, rain, dew, frost, air, sunshine, and breeze will dissolve a foundation of steel if no house is ever built. On faith's foundation, by all diligence, the spiritual superstructure must be reared.

In this passage, the word *"add"* is taken from the leader of a chorus and means to bring forward and supply all things necessary to complete the chorus. We are to *add* to the foundation of faith all things required to make our heavenly character complete and harmonious.

"Virtue" is to be added. Virtue is an eminent endowment, a combination of all virtues, or at least many of them. In this place it means vigor, strength, and power. Courage is a chief and distinguishing idea in virtue.

"Knowledge" is general understanding and intelligence, that instructing knowledge of Jesus and the divine. It involves the intelligent apprehension of divine truths and a thorough conviction of their importance. This knowledge is gained through Scripture by the light of God's Spirit. We are to seek the Spirit of revelation in the knowledge of Jesus. More and more are we to know of Jesus. More and more we are to *"know him, and the power of his resurrection"* (Phil. 3:10). Knowledge is power, strength, and light. We are to be deeply convicted of the truths of religion. We must have a personal knowledge of what the Scriptures teach and an intelligent grasp and apprehension of Bible facts

s far above nature. To prefer others before our-selves in heart and action seems to bewilder and dizzy our untried heads. It is too high. We sigh in despair. We cannot attain it. But faith says, *"I can do all things through Christ which strengtheneth me"* (Phil. 4:13). This crowning of others by uncrown-ing self, this refusing self that others may receive, is grievous to flesh and blood. Who can receive it? And yet it comes to us as a command in the form of law. But New Testament law unfolds the promise and supplies the help to obey. We are to put others before ourselves. This is the complete conquest of self, and it requires a great victory. He who has gained this is worthy to triumph through the gates to heaven!

Pursuing the Heavenly Virtues

Have we learned this lesson and gained this height? Have we received the crown of this grace? Can we in honor prefer another? Has the reign of ambition ceased, the love of the world been destroyed, and has self been crucified? The death of all these must enrich the soil before it can pro-duce this divine fruit.

It is as if God says to His people, "You, by your unwearied diligence, furnish these graces, and I will furnish heaven. You seek these spiritual graces in their abounding fullness, and I will supply to you an abounding entrance into heaven." So, to gain heaven, we must gain these rich graces here. Heaven grows in the soil of the God-prepared

and truths. Light and wisdom in the inner man are to be added day by day as lessons for heaven's graduating day.

"Temperance" follows, and this word's meaning is not limited to intoxicants. It means self-govern-ment. We have learned about ourselves through knowledge; self-control bears its fruit of heavenly wisdom. The tempers, passions, appetites, and desires are all held in by the strong reins of temper-ance. Intemperance cannot enter heaven. Desires are to be limited, as well as appetites and passions. A person may be in excess because of his desires after money, business success, and pleasures. We must be self-governed for God and trained in the school of temperance for heaven.

"Patience" combines with these other graces to perfect in us the Christian character and fit us for the heavenly life. In this noble word there is always a background of bravery. It is the brave patience with which the Christian contends against the vari-ous hindrances, persecutions, and temptations that befall him in his conflict with the inner self and outer world. It is that brave patience that never loses heart or courage, never charges God foolishly, and is not hasty nor revengeful toward others.

"Godliness," God-likeness, brings the heavenly racer into a heavenly atmosphere. He is no longer simply pursuing virtue, knowledge, temperance, and patience, which are principles, facts, and restraints, but he is pursuing the pattern of a person. He is looking heavenward for a pattern

after which to shape his conduct and character. He hears the law speaking through the soft tunes of the Gospel, *"Be ye holy; for I am holy"* (1 Peter 1:16). It is God who speaks, and the struggle for heaven reaches its brightest point when mankind begins to struggle to be like God. Higher relations than earth bind him, higher duties than those to mankind. He is rising to God. He is struggling for God's perfect image, that he may be a reflection of the Divine Person.

He has passed into the divine family. His relation to God gives him a new kinship to mankind. Love is to rule in a family circle. A fellowship has been established, which is the family of God, the union of heaven. *"Brotherly kindness"* is one of the results of our conversion to God and one of the elements of the heavenly life. The fellowship of earth should be like the fellowship of heaven.

Grace has many of the natural virtues. It keeps and polishes these. While not exactly transformed, they are burnished and refined, and adorn humanity with a richness not wholly their own. But grace has distinctive features that separate it from and elevate it above all other virtues. It is original and unrivaled in its super-excellence.

Grace toward One Another

Paul had a masterly and beautiful presentation of the practical side of piety, its most beautiful side; for in no shape is religion so lovely as when in action. Paul described grace in these words: *"Be*

kindly affectioned one to another with broth honour preferring one another" (Rom. 12:1 costly grace; like the most precious gem and only secured with great labor and c is this to be found? Who exemplifies it?

These jewels are readily found in G they adorn almost every page. To tra to practical life among our fallen and m is the chief point of difficulty. To trans sensitive and rare plants, so that they l spread their odor in a strange soil, is and delicate task. These fine spiritual gra seem to be the product of this hurrying values bulk rather than quality. These are ucts of the divine side of our religion, of its divinity. It must have something rude virtues that spring from the soil of l These heaven-induced graces must be see The world demands this before it pays it We are not barren of the ordinary grace only a little to fashion them. But those divinity are rare!

It is the glory of Christianity not onl ent a model of the highest type but also practical illustrations.

"In honour preferring one another." Thi fitly termed the crowning grace. To pl alongside of us is generous and gracious l them before us is divine. To halt so that t catch up would be kindly but to stop and s that others may pass before us in a race f

heart. We seek heaven by seeking these heavenly virtues.

Peter, in concluding this earnest exhortation concerning those graces that fit us for heaven, gave us these words:

> *For if these things be in you, and abound, they make you that ye shall neither be barren nor unfruitful in the knowledge of our Lord Jesus Christ.* (2 Peter 1:8)

To fail in having these heavenly characteristics is to be blind to eternal matters, short-sighted about heaven and all the things pertaining to it, and also to lose what we have already obtained. Past forgiveness amounts to nothing if we do not *"add to"* this initial step the succeeding stages that mark the way to heaven.

"But he that lacketh these things is blind, and cannot see afar off, and hath forgotten that he was purged from his old sins" (2 Peter 1:9). Again this apostle called us to ongoing diligence and the addition of these graces to the sum already secured as the only safeguard from backsliding and final apostasy. *"Wherefore the rather, brethren, give diligence to make your calling and election sure: for if ye do these things, ye shall never fall"* (v. 10).

Then he showed the result of this diligence, toil, and the acquirement of all these divine graces, on heaven: *"For so an entrance shall be ministered unto you abundantly into the everlasting kingdom of our Lord and Saviour Jesus Christ"* (v. 11). Or, as the Revised

Version has it, *"For thus shall be richly supplied unto you the entrance into the eternal kingdom of our Lord and Saviour Jesus Christ."*

> *Let cares like a wild deluge come,*
> *And storms of sorrow fall,*
> *So I but safely reach my home,*
> *My God, my heaven, my all.*

> *There I shall bathe my weary soul*
> *In seas of heavenly rest,*
> *And not a wave of trouble roll*
> *Across my peaceful breast.*

—Isaac Watts

9

The Love Principle

*IN HEAVEN WE SHALL LIVE IN OUR OWN ELEMENT.
WE ARE NOW AS THE FISH IN A VESSEL OF WATER,
ONLY SO MUCH AS WILL KEEP THEM ALIVE. BUT
WHAT IS THAT TO THE OCEAN? WE HAVE HERE A
LITTLE AIR LET IN TO AFFORD US BREATHING, BUT
WHAT IS THAT TO THE SWEET AND FRESH GALES
UPON MOUNT ZION? HERE WE HAVE A BEAM OF
THE SUN TO LIGHTEN OUR DARKNESS AND A WARM
RAY TO KEEP US FROM FREEZING. BUT THERE WE
SHALL LIVE IN THE LIGHT AND BE REVIVED BY ITS
HEAT.* —RICHARD BAXTER

The apostle James said, *"Blessed is the man that endureth temptation: for when he is tried, he shall receive the crown of life, which the Lord hath promised to them that love him"* (James 1:12).

The great condition of this great reward, the crown of life, is love.

It is impossible to overestimate the importance of love. Christ makes it the aim of the moral code and the fulfillment of all prophecy. It is called the royal law and is the fulfillment of that law; the bond of perfection, the test of discipleship, the first of the graces, and the shield on the Day of Judgment.

The thirteenth chapter of First Corinthians shows the meaning of love. We gaze at and admire these words, but rarely do we transfer to practical life this most beautiful and practical of all things. Love is not faith, but it is the only medium through which faith works. It is not hope, though it forms the substance that hope colors and brightens. It is the most common thing, and the rarest. It is often on our lips, but seldom in our hearts; easiest to say and hardest to do.

A Divine Portrait of Love

What is the description given by Paul? Love has passion, but neither envy nor jealousy have any place in that pure flame. It is clothed with humility; neither vanity nor pride inflate its heart or speak from its lips. Unseemly conduct never mars its beauty nor casts suspicion on its fidelity. Love is never provoked to irritation or insulted to bitterness and wrath. It does not suspect ill or avenge wrongs. It is saddened by the triumphs of evil but rejoices in the success of truth. Love is like God in its freedom from hasty and angry excitements and in its long-suffering, self-restraint from evil, mobility toward good, ever-flowing kindness, usefulness, and beneficence.

It has strength to bear, is credulous for good, and is full of hope and cheer for the best. It waits patiently, serene and gentle, when faith, fortitude, and hope have almost failed.

Such is the portrait of this divine love. Such are the principles on which Christ proposes to reconstruct human nature—sublime principles of the Son of God. He proposes to begin and complete His fair and costly building and make His heaven from the material of love.

Christianity is based on this one principle. All else is foreign or false. It is the commandment that completes, aggregates, and dominates the whole; burnished, emphatic, and pregnant with His life and death. The summary of that life and death is, *"Love one another"* (John 15:12). This is the Decalogue revised and completed—the Sinai of Calvary—the law of the Gospel.

Love is the regenerating principle implanted in man's heart by the Holy Spirit. Man must labor with incessant effort and prayer for its perfection.

This love for Jesus, implanted in the renewed heart, has overcome earth's most sacred attachments and become the animating force and crown of our earthly lives. *"Where I am, there ye may be also"* (John 14:3). *"To be present with the Lord"* (2 Cor. 5:8). *"To be with Christ; which is far better"* (Phil. 1:23). *"Father, I will that they also, whom thou hast given me, be with me where I am"* (John 17:24).

To love Jesus is to long to be with Him. To love Jesus is to think about Him. To love Jesus is to obey Him readily and implicitly, not feebly and reluctantly. *"If ye love me keep my commandments....If ye keep my commandments, ye shall abide in my love"* (John 14:15, 15:10). The certainty of heaven is assured when we keep Jesus in the center of our hearts and lives. He is to be the author of impulse and desire, of effort and action. *"Whatsoever ye do in word or deed, do all in the name of the Lord Jesus"* (Col. 3:17).

Results of Overcoming

Will you get to heaven? What is Jesus to you? Does He charm you? Does He draw you heavenward? Do you seek heaven in order to be with Him? Is He the fairest flower in all heaven's garden? Is He the rarest and most precious of all its jewels? Is He sweeter than all its songs? Is He the source of your longings for heaven's blissful abodes? Does the desire to see and be with Him stir the profoundest ambition of your soul?

Jesus and heaven are bound up together. To love Him with an untold passionate devotion is heaven begun, heaven continued, and heaven ended. Paul said,

> *For I am now ready to be offered, and the time of my departure is at hand. I have fought a good fight, I have finished my course, I have kept the faith: henceforth there is laid up for me a crown of righteousness, which the Lord, the righteous judge, shall give me at that day: and not to me only, but unto all them also that love his appearing.* (2 Tim. 4:6–8)

The crown is not only personal to him but universal, only limited to *"all them...that love his appearing."* Here it is not simply love for Jesus personally but love for the great fact that is to culminate in His great glory. To *"love his appearing"* is absolutely necessary for loving His person. Loving His coming is the test of loving His person. We love the fact because we love the person. We are not charged to love any theory or opinion about the manner or time of His coming, but the fact. Let Him come when He will, how He will, and for what purpose He will. We love His coming because we love Him. *"Even so, come, Lord Jesus"* (Rev. 22:20), and bring Your heaven with You.

The overcomers and the conquerors are the heaven-crowned ones. They show valorous strength, undaunted courage, dire conflict, and unyielding steadfastness. They hold fast even to death. By their Christian constancy and courage, they keep themselves unharmed and spotless from all the devices, assaults, and solicitations of the world, the flesh, and the devil. These are crowned to the heavenly life.

They have gained the victory over the devil. *"I write unto you, young men, because ye have overcome the wicked one"* (1 John 2:13). They have overcome the spirit of antichrist.

> *For whatsoever is born of God overcometh the world: and this is the victory that overcometh the world, even our faith. Who is he that overcometh the world, but he that believeth that Jesus is the Son of God?* (1 John 5:4–5)

"He that overcometh shall inherit all things; and I will be his God, and he shall be my son" (Rev. 21:7). Blessed company! They all are "clothed with white robes, and palms in their hands" (Rev. 7:9). They are the victors. The conflict is past, the battle has been fought, and the victory has been won and won forever. They are "more than conquerors through him that loved us" (Rom. 8:37). The blessed Jesus has always led them in triumph, and now they are with Him upon His throne in their last and great triumph.

This love is born of the Spirit of God and is centered on Jesus Christ. Heaven depends on our love to the Savior of sinners. We love heaven only as we love Him and as we seek for Him. This love is to be ardent and supreme. Jesus is the joy and glory of heaven.

Do not I love thee, O my Lord?
Then let me nothing love;
Dead be my heart to every joy,
When Jesus cannot move.

Thou know'st I love thee, dearest Lord,
But O, I long to soar
Far from the sphere of mortal joys,
And learn to love thee more!

10

Looking to Heaven

SALVATION IS THE ONLY NECESSARY THING. THIS CLAY IDOL, THE WORLD, IS NOT TO BE SOUGHT;...CONTEND FOR SALVATION. YOUR MASTER, CHRIST, WON HEAVEN WITH STROKES. IT IS A BESIEGED CASTLE, IT MUST BE TAKEN WITH VIOLENCE. OH, THIS WORLD THIN-KETH HEAVEN BUT AT THE NEXT DOOR, AND THAT GODLINESS MAY SLEEP IN A BED OF DOWN, TILL IT COME TO HEAVEN! BUT THAT WILL NOT DO IT.
—SAMUEL RUTHERFORD

The Christian's attitude toward heaven is one of desire. Paul put it thus: *"For I am in a strait betwixt two, having a desire to depart, and to be with Christ; which is far better"* (Phil. 1:23). Paul's attitude was to long for heaven and desire to be with Jesus.

Jesus has His very best for His disciples. God gives Jesus the key to everything, and Jesus turns everything over to His followers. This ought to kindle and inflame desire. We cannot move heavenward with a chilled heart, a cold purpose, or a frigid resolution.

> *For in this we groan, earnestly desiring to be clothed upon with our house which is from heaven: if so be that being clothed we shall not be found naked.* (2 Cor. 5:2–3)

It is, it must be, an earnest desire. We start toward heaven with a spark, and it ought to be fanned to an intense flame at each step.

The Christian's attitude desires heaven, not to die, but merely to be unclothed of the present. The proper desire is not simply to get rid of the burden of these tentlike bodies. It is not death, for death has no charms for the true Christian. He doesn't fear to die or to live. For him, life has few charms apart from heaven. Death has no charms aside from heaven.

Paul expressed the attitude in these words:

> *For we that are in this tabernacle do groan, being burdened: not for that we would be unclothed, but clothed upon, that mortality might be swallowed up of life.* (2 Cor. 5:4)

This supposes a desire so full of light, expectation, and longing that it is a burden. Heaven is so full of charms to the unclouded vision of faith, so bright and deathless under the rosy hues of an immortal hope, that the present burdens become an intolerable load. To stay is to live in the graveyard, to have a home in a decaying house, to be dying.

Earth is a vast cemetery. Everything foreshadows and breathes death. The desire for heaven is kindled at the fountain of life, where we become sick of the dead and dying. The soul, having tasted of the spring of life, longs to bathe in its full river and yearns to plunge in its immeasurable ocean.

The attitude for heaven is the desire for life rather than death. Here death reigns, imprisons, and ruins. There life reigns, emancipates, and enriches. We are impatiently patient for life eternal—life that is found nowhere else but in heaven. Sick of death, we aspire to life by living and longing for heaven. This groaning for heaven is not natural by earthly standards. The Holy Spirit changes our nature and fashions us for heaven. *"Now he that hath wrought us for the selfsame thing is God, who also hath given unto us the earnest of the Spirit"* (2 Cor. 5:5).

God has fashioned us for this heavenly life. He implants in us these heavenly desires. When we look and long for heaven, these are the marks of God's hand, the results of His work of grace in our hearts. He puts the Holy Spirit in us to keep our memories charged with and alive to the fact of heaven, to keep our desires ardent for heaven, and to keep our hands busy and our tastes sweet for heaven. God works this mighty heavenly work in us so that we will not look at things that are temporal, value things that are insipid and transitory, or strive after the perishing things of earth.

These are material times. Material times always exalt earth and degrade heaven. True Christianity always diminishes earth and augments heaven. If God's watchmen are not brave, vigilant, and sleepless, religion will catch the disease of the times and think little of and struggle less for heaven.

God makes much of heaven. He was the architect and builder of its magnificence and glory. It is His dwelling place, His city by preeminence, His capital, His metropolis, and the home of His family of earthly elect. God fashions every child of His after the pattern of heaven, feeds every child of His on its food, trains every soldier of His for its warfare, and produces in every child of His insatiable thirstings for heaven. When the taste is dull heavenward and the eye dim, then the luster of God has faded from the spirit, the work of God is checked in the soul, the life of God pulsates feebly, and the love of God is chilled to the heart.

"For the selfsame thing"— this heavenly fashion, these heavenly tastes, and heavenly longings—said the apostle, *"is God, who also hath given unto us the earnest of the Spirit"* (2 Cor. 5:5). Not only does this work of God shape and mold us after heaven, but the true work of God in us gives a foretaste and pledge of the heavenly.

To the true Christian, heaven is not a mere sentiment, poetry, or a dreamland, but real, solid, abiding, granite in strength, and home-drawing in sweetness and influence. God is never happier, never better to His earthly saints, than when their heavenly trend is strongly marked. Heavenly longings are plainly and emphatically declared by saints whose devotion to heaven has estranged them from earth. He is not ashamed to be called their God. He has prepared a city for them. What does God think of those who have no sighings for heaven and no longings for it? God's throne is in heaven. His power, person, and glory are preeminently there. Does God attract and hold us? Then heaven attracts and holds. Do we thirst after God?

Jerusalem, my happy home!
Name ever dear to me!
When shall my labors have an end,
In joy and peace, and thee?

When shall these eyes thy heaven-built walls
And pearly gates behold?
Thy bulwarks with salvation strong,
And streets of shining gold?

O when, thou city of my God,
Shall I thy courts ascend,
Where congregations ne'er break up,
And Sabbaths have no end?

11

Racing Down the Stretch

GOD WILL MANAGE OUR AFFAIRS IF WE ARE FILLED WITH HIS AFFAIRS. BE SURE YOU ARE IN GOD'S HANDS AND NOT THAT OF AN ECCLESIASTICISM. I AM VERY FEEBLE. I WANT TO LIVE FOR GOD AND TO DEPART AND BE WITH CHRIST. I HAVE AN UNSPEAKABLE DESIRE TO KNOW THE FUTURE, TO SEE IT AND ENJOY IT, AND TO BE THERE TO SEE AND ENJOY. LET US HOLD ON TO GOD.
—E. M. BOUNDS

The Christian is on a stretch for heaven. With all his power taxed and strained in movement, he is in a race for heaven.

Know ye not that they which run in a race run all, but one receiveth the prize? So run, that ye may obtain. And every man that striveth for the mastery is temperate in all things. Now they do it to obtain a corruptible crown; but we an incorruptible. I therefore so run, not as uncertainly;

so fight I, not as one that beateth the air: but I
keep under my body, and bring it into subjection:
lest that by any means, when I have preached to
others, I myself should be a castaway.

(1 Cor. 9:24–27)

Here we have the picture of the heavenly athlete putting forth all his trained strength to win the prize of an incorruptible crown. The Greek athlete, in his exertion to win the corruptible crown, is a favorite Bible illustration used to stir men for heaven. The athlete has no eye but for the crown. Every part and particle of his strength is put under strain to secure that end. Similarly, we are charged to *"so run, that [we] may obtain."*

Jesus impressed the same idea on the multitude in reply to the question: *"Are there few that be saved?"* (Luke 13:23). Jesus replied as follows: *"Strive to enter in at the strait gate: for many, I say unto you, will seek to enter in, and shall not be able"* (v. 24). *"Strive"* means to agonize. It is the word for intensity of effort—effort that involves the outlay of the fullest strength in an earnest and impassioned way.

Running to Win

Hebrews declares that heaven is gained only by the most intense and persistent effort, which taxes all the strength and demands all possible energy to secure it. Former winners are represented as having gained the prize and arranged themselves as spectators of the renowned and exciting conflict. Jesus Christ, having passed over and marked the way, is seated at the goal to judge the race and award the crown. The racers are charged most solemnly:

> *Wherefore seeing we also are compassed about with so great a cloud of witnesses, let us lay aside every weight, and the sin which doth so easily beset us, and let us run with patience the race that is set before us, looking unto Jesus the author and finisher of our faith; who for the joy that was set before him endured the cross, despising the shame, and is set down at the right hand of the throne of God.* (Heb. 12:1–2)

Where in all the pages of literature could there be a stronger call to throw all energy and weight into the conflict? The issue centers on the racer and his ability to run, to outstrip and to lay aside all things that embarrass or impede progress. Heaven is staked on the race. An incorruptible crown is the reward of successful running. Immortality and eternal life hang on the issue.

Paul charged Timothy to be on the same stretch for heaven. People will not be on the stretch for heaven if their preachers are not so. Paul desired Timothy to lay himself out in the race, to *"fight the good fight of faith"* (1 Tim. 6:12). The word *"fight"* implies intense effort and agony.

Paul also wrote to Timothy about the love of money and its pernicious and damning results. Then he charged Timothy to flee these things.

As worldly men desire and toil after money and so eagerly pursue after it in order to accumulate earthly riches, so Timothy, as a man of God, was to agonize and labor, not for earth and its money but for heaven and its inestimable and imperishable riches.

Paul's Race

In his epistle to the Philippians, we have a vivid view of Paul on a stretch for heaven:

> *That I may know him, and the power of his resurrection, and the fellowship of his sufferings, being made conformable unto his death; if by any means I might attain unto the resurrection of the dead. Not as though I had already attained, either were already perfect: but I follow after, if that I may apprehend that for which also I am apprehended of Christ Jesus. Brethren, I count not myself to have apprehended: but this one thing I do, forgetting those things which are behind, and reaching forth unto those things which are before, I press toward the mark for the prize of the high calling of God in Christ Jesus. Let us therefore, as many as be perfect, be thus minded: and if in any thing ye be otherwise minded, God shall reveal even this unto you.* (Phil. 3:10–15)

Paul purposed to win heaven, not by his marvelous conversion or high apostolate, but by striving for heaven all his life. He was on a stretch for heaven. With all the energy of his imperial nature, ardor, and intensity he could command, *"forgetting those things which are behind,"* he pressed forward with eagerness and strength.

"Reaching forth unto those which are before" means stretching forward in eagerness, energy, and being intensive of pursuit. *"I press toward the mark"* is the figure of running with swiftness and an undying energy. All this indicates an engaging and absorbing interest and effort. It shows a will to persevere in order to hold the whole being in its fullest concentration of strength to gain the end.

Paul, the great apostle, was on the full stretch for heaven. He could not afford to miss its glories.

> *I therefore so run, not as uncertainly; so fight I, not as one that beateth the air: but I keep under my body, and bring it into subjection: lest that by any means, when I have preached to others, I myself should be a castaway.*
>
> (1 Cor. 9:26–27)

Thus he expressed his feelings and purpose.

An apostle, even if he is the chief one, can only make sure of heaven by racing after it always and everywhere. May this example stir us to the profoundest depths. *"Brethren, be followers together of me, and mark them which walk so as ye have us for an ensample"* (Phil. 3:17).

Racers of Christ, arise,

Stand forth, prepare to run:

Toward the goal lift up your eyes,
And manfully go on.

'Tis true the race is short,
But then it is not long;
Each racer soon will take his harp,
And warble Zion's song.

12

To Know Is to Love

*FASTEN YOUR GRIPS FAST ON CHRIST. LET NOT THIS
CLAY PORTION OF EARTH TAKE UP YOUR SOUL....YE
ARE A CHILD OF GOD. THEREFORE, SEEK YOUR
FATHER'S HERITAGE. SEND UP YOUR HEART TO SEE
THE DWELLING HOUSE AND FAIR ROOMS IN THE NEW
CITY. FIE, FIE, UPON THOSE WHO CRY, "UP WITH THE
WORLD, AND DOWN WITH CONSCIENCE AND HEAVEN."*
—SAMUEL RUTHERFORD

The Christian's attitude to heaven is one of knowledge. *"For we **know** that if our earthly house of this tabernacle were dissolved, we have a building of God, an house not made with hands, eternal in the heavens"* (2 Cor. 5:1, emphasis added).

The Christian is as certain of death as any living person. His body is a frail, fleeting Arab tent. He is the heir of death and is hastening to decay. But the Christian knows that *"if our earthly house...were dissolved, we have a building of God, an house not made with hands, eternal in the heavens."*

The Christian has real knowledge about heaven, not a mere wish, hope, or happy guess, but assured knowledge, a fact communicated, and knowledge imparted. God has committed Himself in the strongest way to give knowledge and assurance of heaven to each of His children. The Spirit himself bears witness to our adoption and heirship. (See 1 John 5:6.)

Sealed by the Spirit

In regard to this great fact of our names being written in the Book of Life, we are not left in ignorance. God seals us with the Holy Spirit, who is the *earnest* as well as a witness. A witness bears testimony. The *earnest* is both the pledge of heaven and its foretaste. The Christian believer has heaven in conscious realization, though perhaps not in full measure. The true Christian is no agnostic. He knows some things.

Heaven in this life is not to him as large a reality, but it is as much a reality as it will be when his feet are on the gold pavement of the heavenly city. Heaven pervades and sweetens his whole life. His faith brings to him the very substance of things hoped for, and his hope makes the present luminous by its light and strong by its strength.

Christian faith and hope make the things of heaven real, conscious, and tangible. The knowledge of his home in heaven defies death, change, and misfortune. How attractive that knowledge makes it! A *"building of God...eternal in the heavens"* (2 Cor. 5:1)!

Human hands poison our fairest earthly homes with decay. The touch of human hands has defiled them. Death awaits them. Our palace across the river draws us without regret, but instead with delight, away from our earthly tent, our clay hut. The one who has not anticipated on earth the reality and joy of heaven has had but little of God and none of the sweets of faith.

Are we to be tossed in uncertainty as to our home on high? Is there no assurance? Yes, we know. The Word of God tells us. The Spirit of God has spoken it to our hearts and has left heaven's sweetness and picture there. We have been examining our title deeds lately. They are heavenly deeds, signed and sealed. The house is built, the lot is numbered, all named in our bond, and *"we know that if our earthly house of this tabernacle were dissolved, we have a building of God, an house not made with hands, eternal in the heavens"* (2 Cor. 5:1).

Death makes no pauper of the Christian. It only brings him to his inheritance. Death is the best thing that can come to a Christian. It puts him in possession of his great fortune and brings him to his home. We ought never to sigh; we should go through with radiance and triumph. We ought, always and everywhere, like the saints of old, to take *"joyfully the spoiling of* [our] *goods, knowing in* [ourselves] *that* [we] *have in heaven a better and an enduring substance"* (Heb. 10:34).

Thine earthly Sabbaths, Lord, we love;
But there's a nobler rest above:
To that our lab'ring souls aspire,
With ardent pangs of strong desire.

No more fatigue, no more distress;
Nor sin nor hell shall reach the place;
No sighs shall mingle with the songs
Which warble from immortal tongues.

No rude alarms of raging foes;
No cares to break the long repose;
No midnight shade, no clouded sun,
But sacred, high, eternal noon.

O long-expected day, begin;
Dawn on these realms of woe and sin:
Fain would we leave this weary road,
And sleep in death, to rest with God.

13

Citizenship of Heaven

Love heaven. Let your heart be in it. Up, up and visit the new land and view the fair city, and the white throne and the Lamb—run fast for it is late. —Samuel Rutherford

The Bible puts our citizenship in heaven by such a naturalization force that we are expatriated from earth. We have the sighings of an exile for his native land and the weariness, longings, and loneliness of pilgrims and strangers. The Bible puts all true Christians in the attitude of groaning after heaven. To them, the only life is to live for and in heaven.

The term *heaven* signifies a place of exaltation and glory. It is God's dwelling place. The immediate presence of God is there. It is the land of a higher order of beings and things than exist on earth. It is called *"the third heaven"* (2 Cor. 12:2) because of its loftiness and supremacy, in contrast with the lower heavens.

The good man lays up his treasures in heaven and constantly fixes his heart and eye on them. Heaven is the place where Jesus has gone, where He is preparing a place for us. Heaven is a place, a land very dear to the Christian's heart. The heart beats quicker and the eye grows brighter at the mention of it. The eye of faith holds heaven in sight, and the prayer of faith is lifted to it. Our Father dwells there. Jesus came from heaven on His great mission. The Holy Spirit came down from heaven. The spirits of all the holy dead are there. Heaven is a holy and happy place. An innumerable company is there, safe, blessed, tearless, and immortal.

Heaven ought to draw on our hearts and lift us above earth. It should fill our thoughts and brighten our hopes. Heaven ought to assuage our griefs, banish our fears, lift care from our hearts, and make us immune to the ills of this life.

Jesus was ever lifting His eyes and heart to heaven and ever speaking and thinking of His Father in heaven, so that, supported by its sight and joy, He might endure the cross and despise the shame. (See Hebrews 12:2.) We also should make much of heaven. It ought to be the land in which we live; its atmosphere should surround us, its glories allure us, and its deathless beauties fill our eyes and hearts. It should be the aim of our lives, the goal of our ambitions, the stimulant of every exertion. Our names should be written there, our treasures laid up there.

Heaven in symbol is native land, fatherland, and home. *"For our conversation is in heaven; from whence also we look for the Saviour, the Lord Jesus Christ"* (Phil. 3:20).

In the Revised Version the word *"conversation"* changes to *"citizenship,"* and the note in the margin says "commonwealth." The word has to do with a state or a commonwealth—its laws, regulations, and citizens.

"To day," Jesus said to the dying thief, *"shalt thou be with me in paradise"* (Luke 23:43). Paul said he *"was caught up into paradise"* (2 Cor. 12:4), the paradise of God, a place enclosed and beautiful like Eden, the home of our first parents. The name is transferred to the abode of the saints in heaven, which is called the *"paradise of God"* (Rev. 2:7). The first paradise was made for man, with every tree that is pleasant to the eye and good for food. Beauty, purity, and innocence were there. These all will be in the second paradise in larger proportion.

In the first paradise, *"the LORD God planted a garden"* (Gen. 2:8). In the second paradise, *"He hath prepared for them a city"* (Heb. 11:16). The contrast and progression are from a garden to a city. The first was man's paradise. The second, the *"paradise of God."* Man was in the first paradise. God is in the second paradise. God visited the first paradise. He dwells in the second paradise!

Heaven involves the common well-being and happiness of all people, not just of any favored caste or class. There is a perfect government in which the well-being and happiness of each and all are secured and enjoyed to the fullest measure.

In our previous verse from Philippians, the idea of heaven as a place is emphasized: *"heaven; from whence also we look for the Saviour"* (Phil. 3:20). Jesus, with His human body, must occupy a place, and that place is heaven. We look for Him to come from heaven and do His work of raising the dead and changing the bodies of His saints.

> *Who shall change our vile body, that it may be fashioned like unto his glorious body, according to the working whereby he is able even to subdue all things unto himself.* (Phil. 3:21)

The Christian has his citizenship in heaven. His allegiance is to God, his loyalty is to heaven. He is bound to obey the laws of heaven. The best citizen of heaven is the best citizen of earth. He is bound by highest obligations to obedience, virtue, and government. How exalted are the citizens of such a divine commonwealth!

In the days of Rome's power, the words "I am a Roman" carried with them dignity, honor, safety, and sacredness. "I am a citizen of heaven" ought to represent dignity, nobility, purity, and heavenliness to the fullest measure.

> *O Paradise! O Paradise!*
> *I want to sin no more,*
> *I want to be as pure on earth*
> *As on thy spotless shore;*

O Paradise! O Paradise!
I greatly long to see
The special place my dearest Lord
In love prepares for me;

Lord Jesus, King of Paradise,
O keep me in Thy love,
And guide me to that happy land
Of perfect rest above.

14

Heaven, a Home

⁓

HEAVEN IS CALLED A KINGDOM FOR ITS IMMENSE GREATNESS, AND A CITY BECAUSE OF ITS GREAT BEAUTY AND POPULATION. IT IS FULL OF INHABITANTS OF ALL NATIONS, WHERE ARE MANY ANGELS, AND AN INFINITE NUMBER OF THE JUST, EVEN AS MANY AS HAVE DIED SINCE THE DEATH OF ABEL. AND THITHER SHALL REPAIR ALL SUCH AS SHALL DIE IN CHRIST TO THE END OF THE WORLD; AND AFTER THE GENERAL JUDGMENT SHALL THERE REMAIN FOREVER INVESTED IN THEIR GLORIOUS BODIES. HOW HAPPY WILL IT BE TO LIVE WITH SUCH PERSONS.
—JEREMY TAYLOR

Speaking of Old Testament saints, Hebrews says,

These all died in faith, not having received the promises, but having seen them afar off, and were persuaded of them, and embraced them, and confessed that they were strangers and pilgrims on the

> *earth. For they that say such things declare plainly*
> *that they seek a country.*   (Heb. 11:13–14)

The Revised Version reads, *"For they that say such things make it manifest that they are seeking after a country of their own."*

The English word *"country"* does not portray the idea strongly enough. The word is defined as one's native country, one's fatherland, one's own country. Heaven is our home, our fatherland. Here we are foreigners, pilgrims, and strangers. The loneliness and longing of a stranger and the weariness of the pilgrim should be ours. Our heart-sighing and exiled yearnings should declare to all that we are not at home. It should declare that we are not native to these skies but heaven-born, seeking the heavenly country.

Heaven ought to draw and engage us. Heaven ought to so fill our hearts and hands, our manner and our conversation, our character and our features, so that all would see that we are foreigners, strangers to this world, and natives of a nobler land. We must be out of tune, out of harmony, and out of course with this world. The very atmosphere of this world should be chilling and noxious to us, its suns eclipsed and its companionship dull and insipid. Heaven is our native land and home. For us, death is not the dying hour but the birth hour. Heaven should kindle desire and draw us upward to the skies like a magnet. Inexorable duty to God alone should hold us here on earth.

A beautiful, gifted young woman once said that for several years she had not had a minute when she desired to live one moment longer for the sake of any other good in life but doing right, living for God, and doing what might be to His glory.

Paul was torn between desire and duty. Christ and heaven had his heart, but duty kept him in exile.

> *For to me to live is Christ, and to die is gain. But if I live in the flesh, this is the fruit of my labour: yet what I shall choose I wot not. For I am in a strait betwixt two, having a desire to depart, and to be with Christ; which is far better: nevertheless to abide in the flesh is more needful for you. And having this confidence, I know that I shall abide and continue with you all for your furtherance and joy of faith.* (Phil. 1:21–25)

With Paul, life was as it should be. Duty retires desire and teaches it to wait until the glad hour of its fruition.

Those ancient believers in Hebrews 11 discovered that they were pilgrims and strangers on the earth with heavenly longings and heavenly seeking. (Alas, for the hearts that are settled here; heaven to them is a strange, far-off land.) These pilgrims had left the earth-land and refused to go back to it. They had transferred their home and their homeland to the better heavenly country. God heard their sighing and noted their fidelity and seeking. He was not ashamed of them but built a city for them. It is God-built; that assures its location, glory, eternity, and bliss.

In writing to the Corinthians of the Christian attitude toward heaven, Paul said, *"We are confident, I say, and willing rather to be absent from the body, and to be present with the Lord"* (2 Cor. 5:8). Here we have one of the strongest, sweetest, most attractive symbols of heaven. Whatever there is in that place we call home—sacred, dear, restful, delightful, holy feelings, and deathless ties—all these will be present ten thousand fold stronger and sweeter in heaven.

At home in heaven! What welcome! What satisfaction! What rest to tired feet and tired hearts! What a sense of security and confidence! Nowhere on earth's green, glad soil will the home feeling be so profound, so satisfying, so restful, and so joyful as in heaven. Not only will we realize heaven as home when we get there, but heaven will draw and bind us to itself all along the way. Homesickness for heaven alienates us from earth and makes us wish for our true home.

With deep spiritual insight and the soundest spiritual philosophy, one of Scotland's most gifted and saintly preachers said, after visiting a beautiful Manse, "The Manse is altogether too sweet. Other men could hardly live there without saying, 'This is my rest.' I don't think ministers' manses should ever be so beautiful."

This is not spiteful or overdrawn, but it is the assertion that we must guard against this great peril. Great earthly attachments lessen heavenly attachments. The heart that indulges itself in great earthly loves will have less for heaven. God's great work (often His most afflictive and chastening work) is to unfasten our hearts from earth and fasten them to heaven. He must destroy our infatuation with our earthly homes so that we seek a home in heaven.

My heavenly home is bright and fair:
Nor pain nor death can enter there;
Its glittering towers the sun outshine;
That heavenly mansion shall be mine.

Let others seek a home below,
Which flames devour, or waves o'erflow,
Be mine the happier lot to own
A heavenly mansion near the throne.

—William Hunter

15

Triumph through Triumph Tribulation

THERE IS REQUIRED PATIENCE ON OUR PART TILL THE SUMMER FRUIT OF HEAVEN BE RIPE FOR US. IT IS IN THE BUD; BUT THERE BE MANY THINGS TO DO BEFORE OUR HARVEST COME. AND WE TAKE ILL WITH IT, AND CAN HARDLY ENDURE TO SET OUR PAPER-FACE TO ONE OF CHRIST'S STORMS, AND TO GO TO HEAVEN WITH WET FEET....WE LOVE TO CARRY A HEAVEN TO HEAVEN WITH US, AND WOULD HAVE TWO SUMMERS IN ONE YEAR, AND NO LESS THAN TWO HEAVENS. BUT THIS WILL NOT DO FOR US; ONE (AND SUCH A ONE!) MAY SUFFICE US WELL ENOUGH. CHRIST GOT BUT ONE ONLY, AND SHALL WE HAVE TWO?
—SAMUEL RUTHERFORD

The hatred and persecution cast upon followers of God goes like a knife to many a saintly heart and makes them men *"of sorrows, and acquainted with grief"* (Isa. 53:3). They are shut out. Heavenly faith is cast out by "religion." No persecutors are so heartless and relentless as religious persecutors. No hatred is so bitter as the world's hatred.

> *If the world hate you, ye know that it hated me before it hated you. If ye were of the world, the world would love his own: but because ye are not of the world, but I have chosen you out of the world, therefore the world hateth you. Remember the word that I said unto you, The servant is not greater than his lord. If they have persecuted me, they will also persecute you.* (John 15:18–20)

But from wherever and whomever these persecutions come, they are meant to purify and mature us. God's people are purged and perfected by them. We are not to be impatient under them. We are not to fight against or murmur at them, but to endure them with sweetness and joy. James said:

> *My brethren, count it all joy when ye fall into divers temptations; knowing this, that the trying of your faith worketh patience. But let patience have her perfect work, that ye may be perfect and entire, wanting nothing.* (James 1:2–3)

This is the process.

Paul's words bring to our minds the same view of trials. Putting Jesus Christ in the forefront, as well as our relation to Him of justification and its rapturous peace as the result of faith, gives us fuller access to Him, a farther vision, and a firmer standing. It brings heaven into full view, with the presence of Christ and the glory of God shining through the door of unclouded, undying hope.

And not only so, but we glory in tribulations also: knowing that tribulation worketh patience; and patience, experience; and experience, hope.
(Rom. 5:3–4)

Every holy principle, precious result, and fragrant sentiment brought to us by faith in Jesus is enlarged by tribulation. Through tribulation, patience is made more patient, enriched in sweetness and in strength. Experience is more firmly fixed, deeper rooted, and made steadfast and immovable. Hope is enlarged in scope and vision, increased in luster, and its foundations are laid in jeweled adornment.

Counting It Joy

"We glory in tribulations." Do we? Can we? Heaven in eye and heart enables us to do this strange work. For tribulations not only polish and garnish our heavenly home, but they add many rooms to its size and many gems to its beauty and value.

In the following verses, Peter left his normal thankless service of "stirring up pure minds by way of remembrance" (see 2 Peter 3:1) and rose to vision, beatitude, and anthem:

Blessed be the God and Father of our Lord Jesus Christ, which according to his abundant mercy hath begotten us again unto a lively hope by the resurrection of Jesus Christ from the dead, to an inheritance incorruptible, and undefiled, and that fadeth not away, reserved in heaven for you, who are kept by the power of God through faith unto salvation ready to be revealed in the last time. Wherein ye greatly rejoice, though now for a season, if need be, ye are in heaviness through manifold temptations: that the trial of your faith, being much more precious than of gold that perisheth, though it be tried with fire, might be found unto praise and honour and glory at the appearing of Jesus Christ: whom having not seen, ye love; in whom, though now ye see him not, yet believing, ye rejoice with joy unspeakable and full of glory.   (1 Peter 1:3–8)

Here they all are—God the Father, Jesus and His resurrection, the Spirit and sanctification, hope, heaven, love, and fiery trials. The trials clarify, refine, and swell the anthems to praise, honor, and glory. Trials have brought heaven into a clearer and nearer vision, perfected faith, purified love, and swelled joy until it becomes unspeakable and full of glory.

"Counting it all joy" (see James 1:2) is not simply resignation. That, as a cardinal virtue and crowning grace, is scarcely recognized as a grace at all in times of robust faith. It is not the grace of folded arms and silent hearts, but it is "count it all joy." It is *"glory in tribulations also"* (Rom. 5:3). Glory in tribulations like you glory in heaven, for they are one and inseparable. Rejoice greatly! Rejoice with *"joy unspeakable and full of glory."* Rejoice in the prospect of heaven.

Glory in infirmities. Paul said, *"Therefore I take pleasure in infirmities, in reproaches, in necessities, in persecutions, in distresses for Christ's sake: for when I am weak, then am I strong"* (2 Cor. 12:10).

The Beatitudes are born here, enlarged to their largest measure and most heavenly joy.

> *Blessed are they which are persecuted for righteousness' sake: for theirs is the kingdom of heaven. Blessed are ye, when men shall revile you, and persecute you, and shall say all manner of evil against you falsely, for my sake. Rejoice, and be exceeding glad: for great is your reward in heaven: for so persecuted they the prophets which were before you.* (Matt. 5:10–12)

Listen to Paul again:

> *For which cause we faint not; but though our outward man perish, yet the inward man is renewed day by day. For our light affliction, which is but for a moment, worketh for us a far more exceeding and eternal weight of glory; while we look not at the things which are seen, but at the things which are not seen: for the things which are seen are temporal; but the things which are not seen are eternal.* (2 Cor. 4:16–18)

How Paul discredits and eases the pang of every pain and persecution! *"Light affliction"*–light in weight and short in time. Affliction is light compared with the *"weight of glory"* and short compared with the *"eternal weight of glory."* Highly prized and invaluable are these afflictions as they *"worketh for us a far more exceeding and eternal weight of glory."* Add this estimate to Christ's words, *"Rejoice, and be exceeding glad: for great is your reward in heaven"* (Matt. 5:12).

But these trials work this exceeding and eternal greatness of reward only if *"we look not at the things which are seen, but at the things which are not seen"* (2 Cor. 4:18). The eyes are taken off the things of earth and placed on the things of heaven.

The reward is sure. The *"far more exceeding and eternal weight of glory"* (v. 17) is ours. When our eyes are on the earth, trials wear into our heart's core, and cause us to lose all the measureless and imperishable good that they bring.

Paul judged between the suffering of this life and the glory of the future life: *"For I reckon that the sufferings of this present time are not worthy to be compared with the glory which shall be revealed in us"* (Rom. 8:18). The saints of old had such a high estimate of heavenly things and such a low estimate of earthly things that poverty enhanced heavenly riches. They *"took joyfully the spoiling of* [their] *goods, knowing in* [themselves] *that* [they] *have in heaven a better and an enduring substance"* (Heb. 10:34).

Peter coupled the two thoughts, suffering and heaven, into a common principle.

Beloved, think it not strange concerning the fiery trial which is to try you, as though some strange thing happened unto you: but rejoice, inasmuch as ye are partakers of Christ's sufferings; that, when his glory shall be revealed, ye may be glad also with exceeding joy. If ye be reproached for the name of Christ, happy are ye; for the spirit of glory and of God resteth upon you: on their part he is evil spoken of, but on your part he is glorified. (1 Peter 4:12–14)

Again Peter, when speaking of the devil, declared the universality of affliction wherever saints are found:

Be sober, be vigilant; because your adversary the devil, as a roaring lion, walketh about, seeking whom he may devour: whom resist stedfast in the faith, knowing that the same afflictions are accomplished in your brethren that are in the world. But the God of all grace, who hath called us unto his eternal glory by Christ Jesus, after that ye have suffered a while, make you perfect, stablish, strengthen, settle you. (1 Peter 5:8–10)

The Chastening Process

Heaven is declared to be God's *"eternal glory."* These are words far beyond the earth's dictionaries. Earth's greatest glory, though a fading one, would stir the mightiest ambition and gratify the loftiest aspiration. But what measure is equal to God's eternal glory? What words can define it? What ambition can compass it? And yet we are called to God's glory—to God's *"eternal glory"*! But it is not to be revealed until we have suffered a while. Oh, happy suffering! Oh, short suffering, indefinable in its shortness and limited in its pain when contrasted with God's eternal glory, which is ushered in by trials.

This chastening process often comes through persecutions from the hands of evil men and devils, yet God holds the outcome in His own hands. Nothing is outside of His power. Nothing is excluded from His control for the good of His children. Whether they are things from the devil or bad men, or the mistakes of good men, *"we know that all things work together for good to them that love God, to them who are the called according to his purpose"* (Rom. 8:28). Persecution and affliction cannot hinder God from pressing His faithful elect ones on until they are glorified.

"All that will live godly in Christ Jesus shall suffer persecution" (2 Tim. 3:12). *"In the world ye shall have tribulation"* (John 16:33). *"If we be dead with him, we shall also live with him: If we suffer, we shall also reign with him"* (2 Tim. 2:11–12). These are principles of the Christ-life. There is no persecuting Roman power now, either pagan or papal. Those fierce and cruel days are gone, perhaps forever, but there are petty persecutions. The world still hates Christ's saints, and a worldly church still ostracizes and bans God's people.

Dr. Adoniram Judson wrote from Burmah to a friend in America:

Remember, I pray you, that word of Brainerd. Do not think it enough to live at the rate of common Christians. True, they will call you uncharitable and censorious, but what is the opinion of poor worms of the dust that it should deter us from our duty? Remember that other word of the same holy man, "Time is but a moment, life a vapor, and all its enjoyments but empty bubbles and fleeting blasts of wind."

Again Dr. Judson wrote, "Let me beg of you not to rest contented with the commonplace religion that is now prevalent."

Yet it is this rising above the commonplace, current religion that gives offense, awakens opposition, and kindles the fires of a petty, yet painful persecution. No person who does not rise above the average piety seeks heaven in a real, honest, successful way.

The apostle Paul charged Timothy to *follow after righteousness, godliness, faith, love, patience, meekness. Fight the good fight of faith, lay hold on eternal life*" (1 Tim. 6:11–12), showing the vital relationship between *"following after"* these things and laying *"hold on eternal life."* Heaven is won by winning the heavenly virtues. Ardent pursuit after the graces that constitute heaven is the only way to pursue heaven with passion and gain the prize. To mature and perfect these graces is to be made ready for heaven.

Patience is one of those fundamental Christian virtues in which we are schooled for the heavenly life. Paul, writing to the Romans, said, *"To them who by patient continuance in well doing seek for glory and honour and immortality, eternal life"* (Rom. 2:7). While on earth, Jesus said, *"In your patience possess ye your souls"* (Luke 21:19). Patience is defined as the grace of holding out, endurance, literally staying, remaining behind, steadfastness. He who is unmoved from his original purpose or from his loyalty to faith and piety by even the greatest trials and sufferings is patient.

Patience is a cardinal virtue in Christian character. Its importance cannot be overrated. It is strong and sweet, the pillar of strength, the adornment of beauty. It does not succumb under suffering. It is self-restrained. It does not retaliate wrongs. It is brave and opposed to cowardice or despondency. It has nothing in common with wrath and revenge. It is a gentle grace of serenity and sweetness expressed through every bruised and bleeding pore. It summarizes gospel power and grace. It is *"the kingdom and patience of Jesus Christ"* (Rev. 1:9).

Patience is born and perfected in trial. *"We glory,"* Paul said, *"in tribulations also: knowing that tribulation worketh patience"* (Rom. 5:3). In James, we have this remarkable demand and statement:

> *Count it all joy when ye fall into divers temptations; knowing this, that the trying of your faith worketh patience. But let patience have her perfect work, that ye may be perfect and entire, wanting nothing.* (James 1:2–4)

Count every trial joy, not simply resignation, but joy and gladness—no part distressful or sad. Count them joy at their coming and joy at their results. This is the way perfection comes—*"perfect and entire, wanting nothing"* (James 1:4), every grace present, and every grace mature. Trials bring perfection, maturity, and fullness. God makes our fruit perfect by perfecting our character, and character is perfected by trial.

There is no doubt about the necessity of patience to win heaven. *"For ye have need of patience, that, after ye have done the will of God, ye might receive the promise"* (Heb. 10:36). *"Let us run with patience the race that is set before us"* (Heb. 12:1). Job is a perfect illustration of patience because he held on to God without a shadow of turning through his many trials. *"The LORD gave, and the LORD hath taken away; blessed be the name of the LORD"* (Job 1:21) is the language of patience in its undisturbed, uncomplaining serenity and sweetness. *"Though he slay me, yet will I trust in him"* (Job 13:15) is the language of patience in its endurance and perseverance.

Impatience is the epidemic sin. Strong people, weak people, sick people, well people, old people, young people—all are impatient. All people try our patience. In light of this, how appropriate the universal injunction, *"be patient toward all men"* (1 Thess. 5:14). Patience is necessary to fruit bearing. They who are ready to be reaped for the heavenly harvest *"keep* [the word], *and bring forth fruit with patience"* (Luke 8:15). This grace seems to be slow, indolent, and always waiting. But though Christian patience is very quiet and often silent, it is never lazy. It is *"not slothful, but followers of them who through faith and patience inherit the promises"* (Heb. 6:12). Heaven is for the patient spirit. Heaven is already possessed by the patient. Has patience possessed us?

> *Who suffer with our Master here,*
> *We shall before His face appear*
> *And by His side sit down;*
> *To patient faith the prize is sure,*
> *And all that to the end endure*
> *The cross, shall wear the crown.*

> *Thrice blessed, bliss-inspiring hope!*
> *It lifts the fainting spirits up,*
> *It brings to life the dead:*
> *Our conflicts here shall soon be past,*
> *And you and I ascend at last,*
> *Triumphant with our head.*

> —Charles Wesley

16

The Hope of Heaven

WHAT WAS THE EARTHLY PARADISE IN EDEN COM-
PARED TO THAT PURCHASED BY THE SECOND ADAM,
WHO IS THE LORD FROM HEAVEN? IT IS A PUR-
CHASED POSSESSION. THE PRICE IT COST THE PUR-
CHASER EVERYONE KNOWS. HAVING PURCHASED IT,
HE HAS GONE TO PREPARE IT, TO SET IT IN ORDER, TO
LAY OUT HIS SKILL UPON IT. O WHAT A PLACE WILL
JESUS MAKE IT—YES, HAS ALREADY MADE HEAVEN.
THE VERY PLACE SHOULD ATTRACT US. —NEVINS

I t is not the bare fact of heaven that we are deal-
ing with now, but the Christian grace of heaven,
which is hope.

There is much delusion in believing a mere
fact. Such belief is sterile and deludes if the fact
is not fashioned into a principle. If the cold facts
of the history of the Gospel do not fertilize the
sweet graces of the Spirit, then they are dead and
deadening. These facts of the Gospel as they exist

in the pages of history, even though the pages are inspired, do not save until they enter into our experience and become the bone and blood of our spiritual lives. The fact of heaven must be believed. The heaven of fact exists all glorious and enduring, but this fact of heaven must enter our experience; and then from this experience hope is born, the twin in beauty, intelligence, and goodness with faith and love.

Living Hope

Hope is a mighty spiritual principle. It is so strong that the apostle Paul centered all the forces of salvation in it. *"We are saved by hope"* (Rom. 8:24). By it all the energetic forces that save come into play. These forces are limp and forceless without hope. Heaven nourishes all the principles of a deep, conscious piety. The Christian never works so well, never suffers so well, never grows so well, as when heaven is in full view of his eyes. It is heaven that gives hope its ripeness, richness, and power. Only the saint who is after heaven with all the ardor and brightness of hope is truly saved. Doubt and fear flee away from such a salvation.

By its characteristics, heavenly hope is distinguished from all false hopes that perish. It is patient. Hope can wait and lose none of its brightness. It can wait with serenity and sweetness and without murmuring and disquietude. It is the *"patience of hope"* (1 Thess. 1:3) that adds to its luster and sweetness. *"But if we hope for that we see not, then do we with patience wait for it"* (Rom. 8:25).

It is termed a *good hope,* joined to everlasting consolation. What can be better than a hope that brings in everlasting consolation, a source of perpetual, unfailing joy? It is also termed a *lively* or *living hope.* (See 1 Peter 1:3.) In this passage, Peter told how this true immortal hope came out of the grave of dead hopes, vitalized and immortalized by the resurrection of Jesus Christ from the dead *"to an inheritance incorruptible, and undefiled, and that fadeth not away"* (1 Peter 1:4). Our hope has the imperishable life of Jesus Christ in it. It is called a blessed and happy hope. It has in it all the Beatitudes and all those qualities that bring joy. It makes us happy and secure.

True Christian hope is only seen by the heart's eye. The Revised Version says, *"The eyes of your heart enlightened, that ye may know what is the hope of his calling"* (Eph. 1:18). Our natural eyes and earthly lights do not show us the *"calling,"* nor do they have vision for *"the riches of the glory of his inheritance"* (v. 18) on which hope feeds and lives.

Hope, though it flourishes by the afflictions of life, is formed of the gentlest and mildest graces. It combines meekness with fear. It is not arrogant, rude, or self-assertive, but is mild, retiring, and reverential. It is a very patient grace. It perseveres, holds on, and is steadfast, strong to wait until its fruition comes and saves from discontent, depression, and weakness.

Faith, Hope, and Love

Hope is one of the three great elements of Christian character. It is united with faith and love in order to give perfection, establish Christian reputation, and awaken thankfulness.

> *We give thanks to God always for you all, making mention of you in our prayers; remembering without ceasing your work of faith, and labour of love, and patience of hope in our Lord Jesus Christ, in the sight of God and our Father.* (1 Thess. 1:2–3)

While faith exhibits itself in active works, love shows itself in exhaustive toil; hope brightens all and bears all, declaring her sisterhood to the other graces by patient waiting. Hope's bright endurance sustains faith mightily, and love gives unfaltering and unfainting courage to hope and faith. They are inseparably united in Christian life.

"And now abideth faith, hope, charity, these three; but the greatest of these is charity" (1 Cor. 13:13). Faith appropriates the grace of God in salvation. Love is the animating spirit of our Christian life, while hope takes hold of the future as belonging to the Lord and to those who are His. The kingdom of God—past, present and future—is thus reflected in faith, love, and hope.

A Reason for Hope

How thoroughly hope saturates the system of the Gospel! It is essential to Christian character!

Many passages in the New Testament show how necessary hope is to Christian struggles.

> *Paul, an apostle of Jesus Christ by the command-*
> *ment of God our Saviour, and Lord Jesus Christ,*
> *which is our hope.* (1 Tim. 1:1)

In this passage, hope centers itself in our Lord Jesus Christ. He is our hope. We hang on Him and center all in Him.

This hope of a glorious Christ and a glorious heaven, a glorious and eternal future, is not a prod-uct of man's nature or despair or the outgrowth of his cheerful spirit, but a spiritual gift.

> *Now the God of hope fill you with all joy and peace*
> *in believing, that ye may abound in hope, through*
> *the power of the Holy Ghost.* (Rom. 15:13)

Hope has its spring and being in God. Founded on faith, it floods the soul with joy and peace. It increases by the presence of the Holy Spirit work-ing in us. Hope abounds more and more as we are filled with all the fullness of God. Paul sum-marized the whole plan of salvation, its mystery, and the glory of its riches: *"Christ in you, the hope of glory"* (Col. 1:27). Where Christ is, there hope springs to its opulent fullness. All is barrenness, death, and despair outside of Christ.

The hope of heaven is not a mere emotion. It is not fleeting, but ever enduring and strong. It burns with a steady, brilliant light. It is not an accident, or merely an accompaniment. It is not a mere incident of the religious life but vital, fundamental, and organic. It goes into the being of vital godliness as an essential principle. It dwells in the Holy of Holies and is the High Priest of the inner sanctuary of the soul. It sanctifies the Lord God, and dwells where He dwells.

> *But sanctify the Lord God in your hearts: and be ready always to give an answer to every man that asketh you a reason of the hope that is in you with meekness and fear.* (1 Peter 3:15)

In hope of that immortal crown
I now the cross sustain,
And gladly wander up and down,
And smile at toil and pain:
I suffer out my threescore years,
Till my Deliverer come,
And wipe away His servants' tears,
And take His exile home.

—Charles Wesley

17

Reunion in Heaven

STRIKE YOUR TENT, O PILGRIM,
GIRD YOUR LOINS AND FOLLOW ON;
SOON YOUR JOURNEY'S ENDED,
'TWILL BRING THEE TO THY GOD.
—CLAUDE L. CHILTON

Deep and positive joy springs from the reunion of the broken and wasted loves and friendships of earth. We will see our friends and associate with them in stronger and more hallowed ties because we have been partners in the tears and toils of earth. The society of heaven stands out in an intense and conspicuous manner. Its crowds, its multitudes, its city all express association; and doubtless, while there will be no selfish and exclusive circles, there will be narrow, closer, select ones within the larger. Paul halts our grief for the dead with these words:

> But I would not have you to be ignorant, brethren,
> concerning them which are asleep, that ye sorrow

not, even as others which have no hope. For if
we believe that Jesus died and rose again, even
so them also which sleep in Jesus will God bring
with him....For the Lord himself shall descend
from heaven with a shout, with the voice of the
archangel, and with the trump of God: and the
dead in Christ shall rise first: then we which
are alive and remain shall be caught up together
with them in the clouds, to meet the Lord in
the air: and so shall we ever be with the Lord.
Wherefore comfort one another with these words.
(1 Thess. 4:13-14, 16-18)

We must not weep in despair over the graves of our loved ones who have left us. Why? Because we have hope. We have hope of meeting them again, and, with them, to meet the Lord and be forever with Him, and forever with them. *"Wherefore comfort one another with these words."* We will see them again. We will know them again. We will be with them forever. These are the points of comfort in the apostle's words. Divine comfort that even here on earth makes us victors over death, takes his sting away, wipes the tears from our eyes, and wreathes our hearts with fadeless hope.

Many are the attractions of heaven, all of which should win us from the vain and dying things of earth. First of all, Jesus, our Great High Priest, is there, the Sun and Center of that heavenly world. There is also the absence of so many things that make earth undesirable—sickness and sorrow, pain and death, and earth's privations, discomforts, and disappointments. But added to all these glorious things that should draw us as a strong magnet to heaven is the blessed hope of a glorious reunion with loved ones who have gone on before.

Not only did Paul give us an intimation of this pleasing prospect, but John showed us the things he saw when *"a door was opened in heaven"* (Rev. 4:1). He told us of those who are in heaven—God, Jesus Christ, the Lamb of God, the angels, and those who *"have washed their robes, and made them white in the blood of the Lamb"* (Rev. 7:14).

Who are among these last named? Think a moment. Look back over life and see in your imagination the faces of friends once loved, who broke away, disappeared from view, and now are *"before the throne"* (v. 15). Perhaps some of these were from your own household. There are some whose vacant chairs are but sad reminders of them, *"absent from the body, and...present with the Lord"* (2 Cor. 5:8).

Where are they? *"Before the throne,"* in God's presence, in intimate association with their Redeemer. They are in heaven itself where they *"serve him day and night"* (Rev. 7:15). Their faces peer at us over the walls of the Celestial City, their eyes look at us in imagination as we gaze heavenward, and their hands beckon to us in our heavenward journey.

Will we ever see them again? Yes, if we are faithful amid tribulation, and if our robes are washed in the blood of the Lamb.

Will we know them in that unseen land of light, liberty, and fullness of joy? By all means! For if Moses and Elijah were recognized on the Mount of Transfiguration, if Stephen knew his Lord as they were stoning him, if the rich man in hell recognized Lazarus and Abraham though they were far off in heaven, then there is no doubt that we will know one another in that land. We will not lose our identity in heaven; we will have the same peculiarities and specific makeup in our entire moral being.

In heaven *"there shall be no more death, neither sorrow, nor crying, neither shall there be any more pain: for the former things are passed away"* (Rev. 21:4).

Oh, the blessed hope of a glad reunion with departed saints in the glory world! How they attract us when we look that way!

What vision of glory! What ecstasy came to the apostle Paul, this saintly man, from his association with Jesus Christ!

Almost unnumbered are the illustrations of a truth so resonant of grace that Jesus Christ, even in this life, is the greatest treasure, the profoundest joy, the most gracious influence that can come to man.

What earthly good can give joy like this? Death robs us of every crown of joy but this! Gold, fame, honor, empire, earthly success—all are silenced in the presence of death, which robs us of all and separates us from all! Only Jesus

Christ can give triumph over death. He holds the keys of death. Joy in Jesus Christ is not withered by death's touch.

Come, let us anew our journey pursue,
With vigor arise,
And press to our permanent place in the skies:
Of heavenly birth, though wand'ring on earth,
This is not the place,
But strangers and pilgrims ourselves we confess.

At Jesus' call we gave up our all;
And still we forego,
For Jesus' sake, our enjoyments below:
No longing we find for the country behind;
But onward we move,
And still we are seeking a country above.

—Charles Wesley

About the Author

Edward McKendree Bounds was born on August 15, 1835, in a small northeastern Missouri town. He attended a one-room school in Shelbyville, where his father served as a county clerk, and he was admitted to the bar shortly before he reached the age of nineteen. An avid reader of the Scriptures and an ardent admirer of John Wesley's sermons, Bounds practiced law until the age of twenty-four, when he suddenly felt called to preach the Gospel.

His first pastorate was in the nearby town of Monticello, Missouri. Yet, in 1861, while he was pastor of a Methodist Episcopal church in Brunswick, the Civil War began, and Bounds was arrested by Union troops and charged for sympathizing with the Confederacy. He was made a prisoner of war and was held for a year and a half before being transferred to Memphis, Tennessee, and finally securing his release.

Armed only with an unquenchable desire to serve God, Bounds traveled nearly one hundred miles on foot to join General Pierce's command in

Mississippi. Soon afterward he was made chaplain to the Confederate troops in Missouri. After the defeat of General John Hood's troops at Nashville, Tennessee, Bounds was again among those who were captured and held until swearing loyalty to the United States.

After the war, Bounds pastored churches in Nashville, Tennessee; Selma, Alabama; and St. Louis, Missouri. It was in Selma that he met Emma Barnett, whom he later married in 1876, and with whom he had three children, one of whom died at the age of six. After Emma's death, in 1887, Bounds married Emma's cousin, Harriet Barnett, who survived him.

While he was in St. Louis, Bounds accepted a position as associate editor for the regional Methodist journal, the St. Louis Advocate. Then, after only nineteen months, he moved to Nashville to become the editor of the Christian Advocate, the weekly paper for the entire Methodist Episcopal denomination in the South.

The final seventeen years of his life were spent with his family in Washington, Georgia, where both Emma and Harriet had grown up. Most of the time he spent reading, writing, and praying, but he often took an active part in revival ministry. Bounds was also in the habit of rising at four o'clock each morning in order to pray to God, for the great cares of the world were always upon his heart. He died on August 24, 1913, still relatively unknown to most of the Christian sphere.

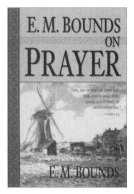

Prayer is the Christian's lifeline to God, and with it lives are changed for eternity! E. M. Bounds knew the secrets of prayer and God's principles for supplying all our needs. Here are his most cherished teachings on the life of prayer, the only effective barrier against the powers of evil so prevalent in this present world.

E. M. Bounds on Prayer
E. M. Bounds
ISBN: 978-0-88368-416-0 • Trade • 624 pages

Guide to Spiritual Warfare
E. M. Bounds
ISBN: 978-0-88368-643-0 • Trade • 160 pages

Forget the image of the devil in a red suit carrying a pitchfork. Here is a very real portrait of a very real enemy, Satan. The Bible depicts the devil as a being of cunning intelligence who is out to derail your faith and your life. Read this book for your own protection so that you can recognize and defeat the strategies of the devil.